CURIOSITIES OF THE AMERICAN STAGE

by

LAURENCE HUTTON

Author of "Plays and Players"

Originally published in 1891.

TO BRANDER MATTHEWS *THESE*

THE ARGUMENT.

This book, as its name implies, is a series of chapters from the annals of the American Theatre; and it considers Plays and Players more particularly in their less familiar aspects. It does not pretend to be critical; and the greatest care has been taken to verify all the facts it contains (many of them here presented for the first time), in order that it may appeal to the small but select band of specialists known as Dramatic Collectors, as well as to those influential members of the community who are glad to call themselves Old Play-goers.

The chapters upon "The American Stage Negro," upon "The American Burlesque," and upon a "A Century of American Hamlets," appeared originally in HARPER'S MAGAZINE; the others have been printed, in part, in other periodicals, but as now published they have all been rewritten, elaborated, and extended.

The portraits with which the volume is enriched are in many instances very rare, and some of them, never engraved before, have been prepared especially for this work. They are from the collections of Mr. J. H. V. Arnold, Dr. B. E. Martin, Mr. Thomas J. McKee, Mr. C. C. Moreau, Mr. Evart Jansen Wendell, and The Players, to all of whom the author here expresses his sincere thanks.

LAURENCE HUTTON.

THE PLAYERS, 1890.

DRAMATIS PERSONÆ.

PAGE

G. W. P. Custis

Edwin Forrest

John McCullough

Major André

J. H. Hackett

Frank Mayo as Davy Crockett

William J. Florence as Bardwell Slote

John T. Raymond

Neil Burgess as the Widow Bedott

F. S. Chanfrau as Mose

Epes Sargent

Anna Cora Mowatt Ritchie

Edgar Fawcett

Brander Matthews

Bronson Howard

Charles Dibdin as Mungo

Ira Aldridge as Othello

Old Play-bill

Andrew Jackson Allen

Barney Williams in *Dandy Jim*

Ralph Keeler

P. T. Barnum

John B. Gough

Thomas D. Rice as Jim Crow

Thomas D. Rice

James Roberts

George Washington Dixon

Mr. Dixon as Zip Coon

Daniel Emmett

Charles White

Edwin P. Christy

George Christy

George Swayne Buckley

Eph Horn

Jerry Bryant

Nelse Seymour

Dan Bryant

Stephen C. Foster

Mrs. Hallam (Mrs. Douglas)

Mark Smith as Mrs. Normer

William Mitchell as Richard Number Three

John Brougham and Georgiana Hodson in *Pocahontas*

Harry Beckett as the Widow Twankey, in *Aladdin*

James Lewis as Syntax, in *Cinderella at School*

George L. Fox as Hamlet

Lydia Thompson as Sindbad

William H. Crane as Le Blanc, in *Evangeline*

Stuart Robson as Captain Crosstree

Harry Hunter as the Lone Fisherman

Francis Wilson in the *Oolah*

Mr. Jefferson and Mrs. Wood in *Ivanhoe*

James T. Powers as Briolet, in *The Marquis*

Charles Burke as Kazrac, in *Aladdin*

N. C. Goodwin in *Little Jack Sheppard*

De Wolf Hopper as Juliet, and Marshall P. Wilder as Romeo

Henry E. Dixey as the Country Girl in *Adonis*

Munrico Dengremont

Josef Hofman

Otto Hegner

Elsie Leslie

Charles Stratton ("Tom Thumb")

Lavinia Warren

John Howard Payne

Blind Tom

Master Burke as Hamlet

May Haines and Isa Bowman as the two Princes in
King Richard III.

Edmund Kean

William Augustus Conway

James William Wallack

William C. Macready

Charles Kemble

Charles Kean

Edwin Forrest

Edward L. Davenport

James Stark

Edwin Booth

Lawrence Barrett

James E. Murdoch

Charles Fechter

Henry E. Johnstone

John Vandenhoff

George Jones

Augustus A. Addams

William Pelby

ACT I.

THE NATIVE AMERICAN DRAMA.

SCENE I.

THE INDIAN DRAMA.

"Do you put tricks upon 's with savages and men of Inde?"

The Tempest, Act ii. Sc. 2.

The American play is yet to be written. Such is the unanimous verdict of the guild of dramatic critics of America, the gentlemen whom Mr. Phoebus, in *Lothair*, would describe as having failed to write the American play themselves. Unanimity of any kind among critics is remarkable, but in this instance the critics are probably right. In all of its forms, except the dramatic form, we have a literature which is American, distinctive, and a credit to us. The histories of Motley and of Parkman are standard works throughout the literary world. Washington Irving and Hawthorne are as well known to all English readers, and as dearly loved, as are Thackeray and Charles Lamb. Poems like Longfellow's *Hiawatha*, Whittier's *Snow-Bound*, Lowell's *The Courtin'*, and Bret Harte's *Cicely* belong as decidedly to America as do Gray's *Elegy* to England, *The Cotter's Saturday Night* to Scotland, or the songs of the Minnesingers to the German Fatherland, and they are perhaps to be as enduring as any of these. Mr. Emerson, Mr. Lowell, and Professor John Fiske are essayists and philosophers who reason as well and as clearly, and with as much originality, as do any of the sages of other lands. In our negro melodies we have a national music that has charms to soothe the savage and the civilized breast in both hemispheres. American humor and American humorists are so peculiarly American that they are *sui generis*, and belong to a distinct school of their own; while in fiction Cooper's Indian novels, Holmes's *Elsie Venner*, Mrs. Stowe's *Oldtown Folk*, Howells's *Silas Lapham*, and Cable's *Old Creole Days* are purely characteristic of the land in which they were written, and of the people and manners and customs of which they treat, and are as charming in their way as are any of the romances of the Old World. Freely acknowledging all this, the dramatic critics are still unable to explain the absence of anything like a standard American drama and the non-existence of a single immortal American play.

The Americans are a theatre-going people. More journals devoted to dramatic affairs are published in New York than in any European capital. Our native actors in many instances are unexcelled on any stage of the world; we have sent to England, to meet with unqualified favor from English audiences, J. H. Hackett, Miss Charlotte Cushman, Joseph Jefferson, Edwin Booth, John S. Clarke, Lawrence Barrett, Edwin Forrest, Miss Mary Anderson, Miss Kate Bateman, Augustin Daly's entire company of comedians, Mr. and Mrs. Florence, Richard Mansfield, and many more; while, with the exception of certain of Bronson Howard's comedies, "localized" and renamed, how many original American plays are known favorably, or at all, to our British cousins? *Rip Van Winkle*, although its scenes are American, is not an original American play by any means; it is an adaptation of Irving's familiar legend; its central figure is a Dutchman whose English is broken, and its adapter is an Irishman. Yet *Rip Van Winkle*, Joseph K. Emmett's *Fritz*, and *The Danites* are the most popular of the American plays in England, and are considered, no doubt, correct pictures of American life.

That the American dramatists are trying very hard to produce American dramas all theatrical managers on this side of the Atlantic know too well, for shelves and waste-paper baskets are full of them to overflowing. Frequent rejection and evident want of demand have no effect whatever upon the continuous supply. How few of these are successful, or are likely to live beyond one week or one season, all habitual theatre-goers can say. During the single century of the American stage not twoscore plays of any description have appeared which have been truly American, and which at the same time are of any value to dramatic literature or of any credit to the American name.

By an original American play is here meant one which is the original work of an American author, the incidents and scenes and characters of which are purely and entirely American. In this category cannot be included dramas like Mr. Daly's *Pique*, or *The Big Bonanza*, for the one is from an English novel and the other from a German play; nor Mr. Boucicault's *Belle Lamar*, or *The Octoroon*, which

are native here, but from the pen of an alien; nor
plays like *Uncle Tom's Cabin*, which are not
original, but are drawn largely, if not wholly, from
American tales; nor plays like *A Brass Monkey* or *A
Bunch of Keys*, which are not plays at all.

The first purely American play ever put upon a
regular stage by a professional company of actors
was *The Contrast*, performed at the theatre in John
Street, New York, on the 16th of April, 1787. It
was, as recorded by William Dunlap in his *History
of the American Theatre*, a comedy in five acts, by
Royall Tyler, Esq., a Boston gentleman of no great
literary pretensions, but in his later life prominent in
the history of Vermont, to which State he moved
shortly after its admission into the Federal Union in
1791. Mr. Ireland and Mr. Seilhamer preserve the
original cast of *The Contrast*, which, however, as
containing no names prominent in histrionic history,
is of no particular interest here. Not a very brilliant
comedy--it was weak in plot, incident, and
dialogue--it is worthy of notice not only because of
its distinction as the first-born of American plays,
but because of its creation and introduction of the
now so familiar stage-Yankee, Jonathan, played by
Thomas Wignell, an Englishman who came to this
country the preceding year. He was a clever actor,
and later, a successful manager in Philadelphia,
dying in 1803. Jonathan, no doubt, wore a long
tailed blue coat, striped trousers, and short
waistcoats, or the costume of the period that nearest
approached this; certainly he whittled sticks, and
said "Tarnation!" and "I vum," and called himself "a
true-born son of liberty" through his nose, as have
the hundreds of stage-Yankees, from Asa Trenchard

down, who have come after him, and for whom he and Mr. Wignell and Royall Tyler, Esq., were originally responsible. Jonathan was the chief character in the piece, which was almost a one-part play. Its representations were few.

This Jonathan is not to be confounded with another and a better Jonathan, who figured in *The Forest Rose*, a domestic opera, by Samuel Woodworth, music by John Davies, produced in 1825, when Tyler's Jonathan had been dead and buried for many years. Woodworth's Jonathan was originally played by Alexander Simpson, and later by Henry Placide. It was long a favorite part of the gentleman known as "Yankee Hill."

The American Drama--such as it is--may be divided into several classes, including the Indian Drama, and the plays of Frontier Life, which are often identical; the Revolutionary and war plays; the Yankee, or character plays, like *The Gilded Age*, or *The Old Homestead*; the plays of local life and character, like *Mose*, or *Squatter Sovereignty*; and the society plays, of which Mrs. Mowatt's *Fashion*, and Bronson Howard's *Saratoga* are fair examples. Of these the Indian drama, as aboriginal, should receive, perhaps, the first attention here.

The earliest Indian play of which there is any record on the American stage was from the pen of an Englishwoman, Anne Kemble (Mrs. Hatton), a member of the great Kemble family, and a sister of John Kemble and of Mrs. Siddons. It is described as an operatic spectacle, and was entitled *Tammany*. Dedicated to, and brought out under the patronage of, the Tammany Society, it was first presented at the John Street Theatre, New York, on the 3d of March, 1794. Columbus and St. Tammany himself were among the characters represented. The Indians who figured upon the stage were not very favorably received by the braves of that day, a large party of whom witnessed the initial performance of the piece; and *Tammany* was not a success, notwithstanding the power of the Kemble name, the good-will of the sachems of the Society, and the additional attraction of the stage-settings, which were the first attempts at anything like correct and elaborate scenic effects in this country.

At the Park Theatre, June 14, 1808, was presented the next Indian play of any importance, and, as written by a native American, James N. Barker, of Philadelphia, it should take precedence of *Tammany*, perhaps, in the history of the Indian drama. It was entitled *The Indian Princess*, was founded on the story of Pocahontas, and, like *Tammany*, was musical in its character. It was printed in 1808 or 1809; the versification is smooth and clear, the dialogue bright, and the plot well sustained throughout.

Pocahontas has ever been a favorite character in our Indian plays. George Washington Parke Custis wrote a drama of that name, presented at the Park Theatre, New York, December 28, 1830, Mrs. Barnes playing the titular part. James Thorne, an English singer, who died a few years later, was Captain John Smith; Thomas Placide was Lieutenant Percy; Peter Richings, Powhatan; and Edmund Simpson, the manager of the Park for so many years, played Master Rolf. Robert Dale Owen's *Pocahontas* was produced at the same house seven years later (February 8, 1838), with Miss Emma Wheatley as Pocahontas; John H. Clarke, the father of Constantia Clarke, the Olympic favorite in later years, as Powhatan; Peter Richings, an Indian character, Maccomac; John A. Fisher, Hans Krabbins; his sister, Jane M. Fisher (Mrs. Vernon), Ann; and Miss Charlotte Cushman, at that time fond of appearing in male parts, Rolf. As these several versions of the story of the Indian maiden are preserved to us, that of Mr. Owen is decidedly the best in a literary point of view. It has not been seen upon the stage in many years. The *Pocahontas* of John Brougham cannot be claimed as a purely American production, and it must be reserved for future discussion and under a very different head.

Unquestionably, Mr. Forrest's great success with *Metamora*, a prize drama for which he paid its author, John Augustus Stone, five hundred dollars-- a large sum of money for such an effort half a century ago--was the secret of the remarkable run upon Indian plays from which theatre-goers throughout the country suffered between the years 1830 and 1840. Forrest, even at that early period in his career, was the recognized leader of the American stage, the founder of a peculiar school of acting, with a host of imitators and followers. Metamora was one of his strongest and most popular parts; its great effect upon his admirers is still vividly remembered, and, naturally, other actors sought like glory and profit in similar roles.

Metamora; or, The Last of the Wampanoags, was

produced for the first time on any stage at the Park Theatre, New York, December 15, 1829. Mr. Forrest, Peter Richings, Thomas Placide, John Povey, Thomas Barry, Mrs. Hilson (Ellen Augusta Johnson), and Mrs. Sharpe were in the original cast. As Metamora Mr. Forrest appeared many hundreds of nights, and in almost every city of the American Union. Wemyss, at the time of the first production of the play in Philadelphia (January 22, 1830), wrote of him and of *Metamora* as follows: "The anxiety to see him crowded the theatre [Arch Street] on each night of the performance, adding to his reputation as an actor as well as to his private fortune as a man. It is a very indifferent play, devoid of interest; but the character of Metamora is beautifully conceived, and will continue to attract so long as Mr. E. Forrest is its representative. It was written for him, and will in all probability die with him." Mr. Wemyss's prophecy was certainly fulfilled. No one after Mr. Forrest's death, with the single exception of John McCullough, and he but seldom, had the hardihood to risk his reputation in a part so well known as one of the best performances of the greatest of American actors; and Metamora and Mr. Forrest have passed away together.

Metamora owed everything to the playing of Forrest; if it had fallen into the hands of any other actor it would no doubt have been as short-lived as the rest of the Indian dramas generally--a night or two, or a week or two at most, and then oblivion. As a literary production it was inferior to others of its class; not equal to *The Ancient Briton*, for which Mr. Forrest is said to have paid the same author one thousand dollars; or to *Fauntleroy* or *Tancred*, dramas of Mr. Stone's, which met with but indifferent success. John Augustus Stone's history is a very sad one; in a fit of insanity he threw himself into the Schuykill, in the summer of 1834, when barely thirty years of age; after life's fitful fever sleeping quietly now under a neat monument containing the simple inscription that it was "Erected to the Memory of the Author of *Metamora* by his friend, Edwin Forrest." With all of his faults and failings, the great tragedian was ever faithful to the men he called his friends.

The Indian of Fenimore Cooper is the father of the stage Indian; and both have been described by Mr. Mark Twain as belonging to "an extinct tribe which never existed." A full list of the Indian plays more or less successful, known in other days and now quite forgotten, would be one of the curiosities of American dramatic literature. A few of them are here preserved:

Sassacus; or, The Indian Wife, said to have been written by William Wheatley, then a leading young man at the Park Theatre, New York, where *Sassacus* was produced on the 8th of July, 1836, Wheatley playing an Indian part, Pokota; his sister, Miss Emma Wheatley, then at the height of her popularity, playing Unca, and John R. Scott *Sassacus*. This latter gentleman, as a "red man of the woods," was always a great favorite with the gallery, and he created the titular roles in *Kairrissah*, *Oroloosa*, *Outalassie*, and other aboriginal dramas with decided credit to himself. In the course of a few years, while the stage-Indian was still the fashion, were seen in different

American theatres *The Pawnee Chief*; *Onylda; or, The Pequot Maid*; *Ontiata; or, The Indian Heroine*; *Osceola*; *Oroonoka*; *Tuscalomba*; *Carabasset*; *Hiawatha*; *Narramattah*; *Miautoumah*; *Outalissi*; *Wacousta*; *Tutoona*; *Yemassie*; *Wissahickon*; *Lamorah*; *The Wigwam*; *The Manhattoes*; *Eagle Eye*; and many more, not one of which lives to tell its own tale to-day.

The reaction against the Indian drama began to become apparent as early as 1846, when James Rees, a dramatist, author of *Charlotte Temple*, *The Invisible Man*, *Washington at Valley Forge*, but of no Indian plays, wrote that the Indian drama, in his opinion, "had of late become a *perfect nuisance*," the italics being his own.

SCENE II.

THE REVOLUTIONARY AND WAR DRAMA.

"List him discourse of War, and you shall hear A fearful battle rendered you in music." *Henry V.*, Act i. Sc. 1.

The first of the purely Revolutionary plays presented in New York was, probably, *Bunker Hill; or, the Death of General Warren*, and the work of an Irishman, John D. Burke. It was played at the John Street Theatre in 1797; and it was followed the next year by William Dunlap's *André*, at the Park.

Mr. Brander Matthews, in his introduction to a reprint of *André*, published by "The Dunlap Society," for private circulation among its members, enumerates a number of plays written shortly after the Revolution upon the subject of the capture and death of the British spy, many of which, however, were never put upon the stage. André had been dead less than twenty years when Dunlap's *André* was first produced, in 1798, and Arnold was still living; and, curiously enough, *The Glory of Columbia*, also by Dunlap, in which Arnold and André both figured, was played at the old South Street Theatre, Philadelphia, in 1807, with scenes painted by André himself, who had superintended amateur theatricals at that house, and had played upon that very stage.

After *Bunker Hill* and *André* came at different periods in New York *The Battle of Lake Erie*; *The Battle of Eutaw Springs*; *A Tale of Lexington*; *The Siege of Boston*; *The Siege of Yorktown*; *The Seventy-Sixer*; *The Soldier of '76*; *Marion; or, The Hero of Lake George*; *Washington at Valley Forge*; and many more of the same stamp--all of which were popular enough during the first half-century of our history, but during the last half they have entirely disappeared.

A play of Revolutionary times which deserves more than passing notice here was *Love in '76*, by Oliver B. Bunce, produced at Laura Keene's Theatre in New York in September, 1857; Miss Keene playing Rose Elsworth, the heroine; Tom Johnstone Apollo Metcalf, a Yankee school-teacher--a part that suited his eccentric comedy genius to perfection; and J. G. Burnett Colonel Cleveland of the British Army, a wicked old soldier, in love with Rose, and completely foiled by the other two in the last act. *Love in '76* was unique in its way, being the only "parlor play" of the Revolution, the only play of that period which is entirely social in its character; and a charming contrast it was to its blood-and-thunder associates on that account--a pretty, healthy little story of woman's love and woman's devotion in the times that tried men's hearts as well as souls. It was not put upon the stage with the care it deserved, and was too pure in tone to suit a public who craved burlesque and extravaganza. It has not been played in some years. Mr. Bunce was the author of other plays, notably the *Morning of Life*, written for the Denin Sisters, then clever little girls, which they produced at the Chatham Theatre, New York, in the summer of 1848. George Jordan and John Winans, the latter a very popular low-comedian on the east side of the town, were in the cast. At the same house, two years later, was played *Marco Bozzaris*, a melodrama in blank verse, with very effective scenes and situations, written by Mr. Bunce, and founded not on Halleck's poem, but on the story of Bozzaris as related in the histories. James W. Wallack, Jr. (then known as "Young Wallack"), was the hero; Susan Denin was his martyred son; John Gilbert was the villain of the piece; and Mrs. Wallack the hero's wife. *Marco Bozzaris* was very popular, and was not withdrawn until the end of the Bowery season.

But to return to the drama particularly devoted to war. *The Battle of Tippecanoe* related to the Indian wars, as *The Battle of New Orleans* was founded on the War of 1812, and *The Battle of Mexico* on our

Mexican difficulties some years later. The contemporaneous literature of the stage inspired by the War of the Rebellion was not extensive or worthy of particular notice. It was confined generally to productions like *The Federal Spy; or, Pauline of the Potomac*, at the New Bowery Theatre, New York, and *The Union Prisoners; or, The Patriot's Daughter*, at Barnum's Museum. During the struggle for national existence war on both sides of the Potomac was too serious a business, and too near home, to attract people to its mimic representations on the stage, and it was not until *Held by the Enemy* and *Shenandoah* were produced, a quarter of a century after the establishment of peace, that American play-goers began to find any pleasure in theatrical representations of a subject which had previously been so full of unpleasantness. These later war dramas, however, are so much superior in plot, dialogue, and construction to any of the plays founded upon our earlier wars, so far as these earlier plays have come down to us, that they may encourage the optimist in theatrical novelties to believe that there is some hope for the future of that branch of dramatic literature at least.

SCENE III.

THE FRONTIER DRAMA.

"Here in the skirts of the forest." *As You Like It*, Act
iii. Sc. 2.

The drama of frontier life in this country may be
described as the Indian drama which is not all
Indian; and even this variety of stage play is fast
disappearing with the scalp-hunter, and with the
Indian himself, going farther and farther to the
westward every year. It may be said to have been
inaugurated by James K. Paulding, a native of the
State of New York, who wrote the part of Colonel
Nimrod Wildfire, in *The Lion of the West*, for J. H.
Hackett, in 1831. Wildfire, afterwards put into a
drama called *The Kentuckian*, by Bayle Bernard,
wore buckskin clothes, deer-skin shoes, and a coon-
skin hat; and he had many contemporary imitators,
who copied his dress, his speech, and his gait, and
stalked through the deep tangled wild woods of
east-side stages for many years; to the delight of
city-bred pits and galleries, who were perfectly
assured that *Kit, the Arkansas Traveller*--and one of
the best of his class--was the real thing, until they
saw Buffalo Bill with actual cowboys and *bona fide*
Indians in his train, and lost all further interest in
The Scouts of the Prairies, or in *Nick of the Woods*,
which hitherto had filled their idea of a life on the
plains.

Only two modern plays of this character are worthy
of serious attention here--Augustin Daly's *Horizon*
and the *Davy Crockett* of Frank E. Murdoch.

Horizon, one of Mr. Daly's earliest works, was
produced at the Olympic Theatre, March 22, 1871,
and ran for two months. In the advertisements it
was called "a totally original drama, in five acts,
illustrative of a significant phase of New York
society, and embodying the varied scenes peculiar
to American frontier life of the present day." It was
certainly an American play. In no other part of the
world are its characters and its incidents to be met
with. Complications of plot and scenery and certain
surprises in the action were evidently aimed at by
the author rather than literary excellence. A
panorama of a Western river and a night surprise of
an Indian band upon a company of United States
troops were well managed and very effective. The
play was suggestive of Bret Harte's sketches and of
dime novels, with its gambler, its Heathen Chinee,
its roughs of "Rogues' Rest" its vigilance
committee, its abandoned wife, and its prairie
princess. The Indian element did not predominate in
Horizon, and was not offensive. The part of
Wannamucka, the semi-civilized redskin, very well
played by Charles Wheatleigh, was quite an original
conception of the traditional untutored savage; he
was wild, romantic, treacherous, but with a touch of
dry humor about him that made him attractive in the
drama, if not according to the nature of his kind.
Panther Loder might have stepped out of the story
of *The Outcasts of Poker Flat*--one of those cool,
desperate, utterly depraved, but gentlemanly rascals
whom Mr. Harte has painted so graphically, and
whom John K. Mortimer could represent so
perfectly upon the stage. Mortimer, during his long
career, never did more artistic work than in this
rôle. The stars in *Horizon* whose names on the bills

appeared in the largest type were Miss Agnes Ethel, the White Flower of the Plains, and George L. Fox. The lady was gentle, charming, and very pretty in a part evidently written to fit her; not so great as in *Frou Frou*, in which she made her first hit, or as *Agnes*, which was to follow; but it was a pleasant, creditable performance throughout. Poor Fox, as Sundown Bowse, the Territorial Congressman, furnished the comic element in the piece; he was humorous and not impossible--the first of the Bardwell Slotes and Colonel Sellerses and Silas K. Woolcotts who are now the accepted stage-Yankees, and who furnish most of the amusement in the modern American drama. Mr. Fox has not been greatly surpassed by any of his successors in this line. Miss Ada Harland as his daughter, Miss Lulu Prior as the royal Indian maiden, Mrs. Yeamans as the Widow Mullins, and little Jennie Yeamans as the captured pappoose all added to the popularity of the play. Taken as a whole, *Horizon* is the best native production of its kind seen here in many years, with the single exception of *Davy Crockett*.

Mr. Frank Murdoch called his *Davy Crockett* a "backwoods idyl." It is almost the best American play ever written. A pure sylvan love-story, told in a healthful, dramatic way, it is a poem in four acts; not perfect in form, open to criticism, with faults of construction, failings of plot, slight improbabilities, sensational situations, and literary shortcomings, but so simple and so touching and so pure that it is worthy to rank with any of the creations of the modern stage in any language. The character of Davy Crockett, the central figure, is beautifully and artistically drawn: a strong, brave young hunter of the Far West; bold but unassuming; gentle but with a strong will; skilled in woodcraft but wholly ignorant of the ways of the civilized world he had never seen; capable of great love and of great sacrifices for his love's sake; shy, sensitive, and proud; unable to read or to write; utterly unconscious of his own physical beauty and of his own heroism; faithful, honest, truthful--in short, a natural gentleman. The story is hardly a new one. Davy seems to be the son of the famous Davy Crockett whose reputation was so great that his very name became a terror to the 'coons of the wild woods, and who left to his children and to posterity the wholesome advice that it is only safe to go ahead when one is sure one is right in going. On this motto the Davy Crockett of the play always acts. He is in love with a young lady who is his superior in station and education. Of his admiration he is not ashamed, but in his simple, honest modesty he never dreams of winning the belle of the county, or that there is anything in him that can attract a refined woman. It is his good fortune to save her life from Indians and from wolves at some risk of his own scalp, and with some damage to his own person. In a forest hut, while she nurses his wounds, she recites to him the story of Young Lochinvar, upholding the course of the borderer of other lands and other days, so faithful in love, so dauntless in war, telling of her own approaching marriage to a laggard in love and a dastard in battle, into which her father would force her. On this hint he speaks, sure he is right at last, and going ahead, like the young hero in Marmion, to win this old man's daughter. He carries her away from the arms of the man she hates; one touch of her hand and one word in her ear is enough; through all the wide border his steed is the best; there is racing and chasing through Cannobie Lee, behind the footlights and in the wings, but Lochinvar Crockett wins his bride, the curtain falls on proud gallant and happy maiden, and the band plays "Home, Sweet Home."

All this, of course, is the old, old story so often told on the stage before, and to last forever; but Mr. Murdoch seems to have told it better than any of his fellow-countrymen.

There is no doubt, however, that *Davy Crockett*, like *Metamora*, owes much of its success to the actor who plays its titular part. Mr. Frank Mayo's performance of this backwoods hero is a gem in its way. He is quiet and subdued, he looks and walks and talks the trapper to the life, never overacts, and never forgets the character he represents. He first played *Davy Crockett* in Rochester in November, 1873, producing it in New York at Niblo's Garden on the 9th of March, 1874, when he had the support of Miss Rosa Rand as Eleanor Vaughn, the heroine who looked down to blush and who looked up to sigh, with a smile on her lip and a tear in her eye, and who made in the part a very favorable impression. The play has never been properly appreciated by metropolitan audiences. Free from tomahawking and gun-firing, it does not attract the lovers of the sensational; utterly devoid of emotional and harrowing elements, it does not appeal to the admirers of the morbid on the stage; and, giving no scope for richness of toilet, it has no charms for the habitual attendants upon matinée entertainments.

Its reception by the press was not cordial or kindly, and the severe things written about it had, it is said, such an effect upon its sensitive author that he literally died of criticism in Philadelphia, November 13, 1872. Frank H. Murdoch was a nephew of James E. Murdoch, the old tragedian, and was himself an actor of some promise. His single play was of so much promise that if there were an American Academy to crown such productions it might have won for him at least one leaf of the laurel.

SCENE IV.

THE STAGE AMERICAN IN THE CHARACTER PLAY.

"What hempen homespuns have we swaggering here?" *A Midsummer-Night's Dream*, Act iii. Sc. 1.

The typical and accepted American of the stage, the most familiar figure in our dramatic literature, is a Jonathan, an Asa Trenchard, a Rip Van Winkle, a Solon Shingle, a Bardwell Slote, a Mulberry Sellers, and a Joshua Whitcomb; and even he does not always figure in the American play as it is here defined.

Jonathan, of whom something has already been said, is now extinct and defunct. Asa Trenchard is the creation of an Englishman (Tom Taylor), brought to perfection by the genius of Mr. Jefferson. Rip Van Winkle, as has been said before, is a Dutchman taken from the pages of Irving's familiar tale, and so accentuated by the genius of this same Jefferson in the present generation, that the fact that he had distinguished predecessors in the same character, but in other dramatizations of the story, is almost forgotten now. Hackett was the original Rip in 1830. Of his performance Sol Smith wrote then: "I should despair of finding a man or a woman in an audience of five hundred who could hear Hackett's utterance of five words in the second act, 'But she vas mine vrow,' without experiencing some moisture in the eyes." The second Rip Van Winkle was Charles Burke, a half-brother of Mr. Jefferson who considers Burke's the best Rip Van Winkle of the trio. He was the author of his own version of the play. Concerning his "*Are we so soon forgot?*" L. Clarke Davis quotes John S. Clarke as saying: "It fell upon the senses like the culmination of all mortal despair, and the actor's figure, as the low sweet tones died away, symbolized more the ruin of a representative of a race than the sufferings of an individual. His awful loss and loneliness seemed to clothe him with a supernatural dignity and grandeur which commanded the sympathy and awe of his audience." Mr. Clarke adds that in supporting Mr. Burke in this part night after night, and while perfectly aware of what was coming, and even watching for it, when these lines were spoken his heart seemed to rise in his throat, and his eyes were wet with tears. The *Rip Van Winkle* which Mr. Jefferson has played so often on both sides of the Atlantic is his own version of the story, somewhat elaborated by Mr. Boucicault; and Mr. Jefferson's Rip Van Winkle is Rip Van Winkle himself.

It was Charles Burke who first discovered the possibilities lying dormant in the character of Solon Shingle, a sort of Yankee juvenile Paul Pry, in a two-act drama called *The People's Lawyer*, by Dr. J. S. Jones. "Yankee" Hill and Joshua Silsbee--both admirable representatives of Yankee character parts--played Solon Shingle as a young man, with all of the "Down-East" characteristics which distinguish stage Down-Easters; and it was not until he fell into the hands of Burke that he became the simple-minded, phenomenally shrewd old man from New England, with a soul which soared no higher than the financial value of a bar'l of apple-sass. Until Mr. Owens, the last of the Solon Shingles, died and took Solon Shingle with him, the drivelling old farmer from Massachusetts was as perfect a specimen of his peculiar species as our stage has ever seen.

Judge Bardwell Slote may be called with justice "a humorous satire," which is the subtitle given by Benjamin Woolf to the play of *The Mighty Dollar*, in which he is found. He is a politician of the worst stamp, with many amiable and commendable qualities. He is vulgar to an almost impossible degree, personally offensive, and yet entirely delightful to meet--on the stage, where Mr. Florence kept him for many hundreds of successive nights. If he never existed in real life--and it is to be hoped for the sake of our national credit that he did not--Mr. Florence made him not only possible but probable.

The Senator, written by David Lloyd, and retouched by Sydney Rosenfeld for Wm. H. Crane, is a native legislator of a somewhat different type. He is an honest politician, who may perhaps be found in the Senate of one of the States of the nation, and even in the Upper House of the nation itself. He is a man of energy and of what is called "snap"; he is full of engagements which he has no time to keep; he is loquacious, of course, for loquacity is part of his business capital; he is loud, self-made, self-educated, self-reliant, and not always refined. His humor is peculiarly American, and in Mr. Crane's hands he is very human.

Mr. Warner and Mr. Clemens, jointly with John T. Raymond, are responsible for the character of Colonel Mulberry Sellers, a stage American from the Southern States. He is quite as much exaggerated as Slote, and quite as amusing. He can be found in part in all sections of the country, perhaps, but as a whole, happily for the country, he does not exist at all, except upon the stage.

The great charm of Joshua Whitcomb is that he is a real man of real New England flesh and blood, so true to the life that when Mr. Thompson took him to Keene, New Hampshire, not very far from Swanzey, his audiences wanted their money back, on the ground that they got nothing for it but what they saw, free of charge, all about them every day. "It

warn't no actin'; it was jest a lot of fellers goin'
around and doin' things." The manner in which Mr.
Thompson goes about in *The Old Homestead*, and
does things, is the perfection of art; and if he is not
the best of his class, it is not because he is the least
natural and the least lovable.

It is a curious commentary upon the rarity of typical
stage Americans of the gentler sex that only two of
any prominence have appeared of late years, and
that these are everything but gentle, and are both
played by a man. Mrs. Barney Williams and Mrs.
Florence were very popular as "Yankee gals" with a
previous generation; but to Neil Burgess must we
turn now for the only correct picture of the women
who are fit to mate (upon the stage) with those
heroes of the stage who fill our rural homesteads
and our legislative lobbies. The Widow Bedott, and
her friend of *The County Fair*, most assuredly are
worthy of equal rights with Joshua Whitcomb and
Bardwell Slote.

SCENE V.

THE LOCAL NEW YORK DRAMA.

"Like boys unto a muss." *Antony and Cleopatra*,
Act iii. Sc. 13.

The number of plays based upon life in New York,

all of which are strangely similar in title and in plot,
or what must pass for plot, and all of which have
been seen upon the New York stage since the first
appearance of *Mose*, will surprise even those most
familiar with our theatrical literature. Taken almost
at random from various files of old play-bills, and
from Mr. Ireland's *Records*, there were *A Glance at
New York; or New York in 1848*; *New York As it Is*;
First of May in New York; *The Mysteries and
Miseries of New York*; *Burton's New York
Directory*; *The New York Fireman*; *Fast Young Men
of New York*; *Young New York*; *The Poor of New
York*; *New York by Gaslight*; *New York in Slices*;
The Streets of New York; *The New York Merchant
and his Clerks*; *The Ship-carpenter of New York*;
The Seamstress of New York; *The New York
Printer*; *The Drygoods Clerk of New York*, and
many more, including *Adelle, the New York
Saleslady*, which last was seen on the Bowery side
of the town as late as 1879.

These were nearly all spectacular plays, and they
were usually realistic to a degree in their
representation of men and things in the lower walks
of life. Rich merchants, lovely daughters, wealthy
but designing villains, comic waiter-men, and pert
chamber-maids with song and dance
accompaniment, were placed in impossible uptown
parlors; but the poor but honest printer set actual
type from actual cases, and cruelly wronged but
humble maidens met disinterested detectives by real
lamp-posts and real ash-barrels, in front of what
really looked like real saloons.

The original of all these local dramas was *New York*

in 1848, or, as it was called during its long run of twelve weeks at the Olympic in that year, *A Glance at New York*. It was a play of shreds and patches, hurriedly and carelessly stitched together by Mr. Baker, the prompter of Mitchell's famous little theatre, in order to cover the nakedness of the programme on the night of his own annual benefit. It had no literary merit, and no pretensions thereto; and it would never have attracted public attention but for the wonderful "B'hoy" of the period, played by F. S. Chanfrau--one of those accidental but complete successes upon the stage which are never anticipated, and which cannot always be explained. He wore the "soap locks" of the period, the "plug hat," with a narrow black band, the red shirt, the trousers turned up--without which the genus was never seen--and he had a peculiarly sardonic curve of the lip, expressive of more impudence, self-satisfaction, suppressed profanity, and "general cussedness" than Delsarte ever dared to put into any single facial gesture. Mr. Chanfrau's Mose hit the popular fancy at once, and retained it until the Volunteer Fire Department was disbanded; and *A Glance at New York* was fol-lowed by *Mose in California*, *Mose in a Muss*, and even *Mose in China*. Mr. Matthews, in an article contributed to one of the magazines a few years ago, records the fact that during one season Mr. Chanfrau played Mose at two New York theatres and in one theatre in Newark on the same night.

The Mulligan Guards, *The Skidmores*, and their followers were the legitimate descendants of *Mose*, and they came in with the steam-engines and the salaried firemen, who took away the occupation and the opportunities of Sykesy and Jake. Harrigan and Hart began their theatrical management at the Theatre Comique, opposite the St. Nicholas Hotel, in 1876, and introduced what may be called the Irish-German-Negro-American play, illustrating phases of tenement-house life in New York, and amusing everybody who ever saw them, from the Babies on our Block to Muldoon himself, the Solid Man. Mr. Harrigan wrote his own plays; both he and Mr. Hart were inimitable in their peculiar line as actors, and they were wise and fortunate in their selection of their company, which included Mrs. Annie Yeamans, "Johnny" Wild, and other equally talented artists, for whom "Dave" Braham, the leader of the orchestra, wrote original and catching music, which was sung and whistled and ground out from one end of the country to the other. Mr. Harrigan is a close observer and a born manager, and his productions have been masterpieces in their way. He puts living men and women upon the stage. He has done for a certain phase of city life what Denman Thompson has done for life upon a farm; and he is more to be envied than Mr. Thompson, because no class of theatre-goers enjoy his productions more than do the living men and women whom his company, with real art, represent. But, alas! his plays are not the *great* American plays for which the American dramatic critic is pining; although, like *The Old Homestead*, and *Shenandoah*, and *Horizon*, and *Metamora*, and *Fashion* they approach greatness, if only in the fact that they have introduced, and preserved, a series of purely American types which are as great in their way as are the dramatic characters of other lands, and greater and more enduring than many of the

Americans to be found in other branches of
American literature.

SCENE VI.

THE SOCIETY DRAMA.

"Full of most excellent differences, of very soft
society, and great showing."--*Hamlet*, Act v. Sc. 2.

A few extracts from the prologue which Mr. Epes
Sargent wrote for Mrs. Mowatt's *Fashion*, in 1845,
will give a comparatively correct picture of the
feeling which existed between native playwrights
and the dramatic critics of this country towards the
end of the first half of the present century, and will
show how strong was the prejudice then existing
against dramatic works of home manufacture. The
comedy was purely original; its writer was an
American, and a woman; its scenes were laid in the
city of New York; and *Fashion* was emphatically an
American play.

At the rising of the curtain on the opening night Mr.
Crisp was discovered reading a newspaper; and he
spoke as follows, the italics being Mr. Sargent's
own:

"*Fashion*, a Comedy! I'll go--but stay-- Now I read
farther, 'tis a *native* play! Bah! home-made calicoes

are well enough, But home-made dramas *must* be stupid stuff. Had it the *London* stamp 'twould do; but then For plays we lack the manners and the men! Thus speaks *one* critic--hear *another's* creed: *Fashion!* What's here? [*Reads.*] It never can succeed! What! from a *woman's* pen? It takes a *man* To write a comedy--no woman can!

But, sir--but, gentlemen--you, sir, who think No comedy can flow from *native* ink-- Are we such *perfect* monsters, or such *dull*, That wit no traits for ridicule can cull? Have we no follies here to be redressed? No vices gibbeted? No crimes confessed?

Friends, from these scoffers we appeal to you! Condemn the *false*, but, oh, applaud the *true*! Grant that *some* wit may grow on native soil, And Art's fair fabric rise from *woman's* toil! While we exhibit but to *reprehend* The social vices, 'tis for *you* to mend!"

The audience was long and loud in its applause of the prologue, but the play was so well written, so well represented, and so deserving of success that Mrs. Mowatt and Mr. Sargent might have spared themselves their appeal to the sympathy of the general public. The critics, as a rule, were well disposed, although Edgar Allan Poe, one of the sternest of them, said that *Fashion* resembled *The School for Scandal*, to which some of its admirers had likened it, as the shell resembles the living locust; a stricture which was hardly just. *Fashion* created an excitement in the theatrical world that had not been known for years before, and has hardly been equalled since. It was said, and with some truth, to have revived the drama in this country, and to have reawakened a declining taste for dramatic representations of the higher and purer kind. It was almost the first attempt made to exhibit on our stage a correct picture of American society and manners, and although it was a satire on a certain *parvenu* class, conspicuous then as now in the metropolis, and always likely to exist here, it was a kindly, good-natured satire that did not intend to wound even when it was most pointed. Several familiar New York types were faithfully and cleverly represented: the millionaire merchant, vulgar, self-made, proud of his maker; and his wife, uneducated, pretentious, devoted to dress and display, seeking to marry her daughter to the adventurous foreigner who is not yet obsolete in the "upper circles" of metropolitan society. There were besides these, in the underplot, a rich old Cattaraugus farmer, his granddaughter (a dependant in the merchant's family), a prying old maid, a black servant, a poet, and a fashionable selfish man of the world. All of these were well drawn and natural. The situations were probable, and had existed and do exist in real life, while the language was bright and pure. The dramatic critic of the *Albion*, then a leading and influential journal, pronounced *Fashion* to be "the best American comedy in existence, and one that sufficiently indicated Mrs. Mowatt's ability to write a play that would rank among the first of the age." Mrs. Mowatt, however, was the author of but one other successful drama, *Armand, the Child of the People*. It was first played at the Park Theatre on September 27, 1847; while *Fashion* itself has not been put upon the stage here in many years, and is almost forgotten, although its influence is still felt. Its popularity endured longer, perhaps, than that of any of its contemporaries; it was played throughout the United States, and was well received by London and English provincial audiences. The oblivion into which it has fallen now should by no means be ascribed to its want of merit, the fashion of the time having changed.

The comedy was produced at the Park Theatre on the 24th of March, 1845. The *Herald* of the next day said it had one of the best houses ever seen in New York; boxes, pit, and gallery were crowded; all of the *literati* of the city were present, with a tolerable sprinkling of the *élite*--the *Herald's* distinction between the *élite* and *literati* might have suggested another satirical play--and the comedy was enthusiastically received. Its initial cast was a very strong one and worthy of preservation. William Chippendale played Adam Trueman, the farmer; William H. Crisp, the elder, was Count Jolimaitre, the fraudulent nobleman; John Dyott was Colonel Howard, of the United States Army, in love with Gertrude; Thomas Barry was Tiffany, the wealthy merchant; T. B. De Walden, author of *Sam*, *The Baroness*, and other plays, was T. Tennyson Twinkle, a modern poet; John Fisher played Snobson, the confidential clerk, and Mr. Skerrett Zeke, a colored servant. None of these gentlemen are known to our stage to-day, but without exception they were as great in the various lines in which they were cast as could then be found in America. In the ladies of its first representations *Fashion* was equally fortunate, and Mrs. Mowatt herself, in her *Autobiography*, writes that she felt

much of the great success of the play to be justly
due to the cleverness of the players. Mrs. Barry--the
first Mrs. Barry, who died in 1854--represented the
would-be lady of fashion; Miss Kate Horn (Mrs.
Buckland), Seraphina Tiffany, her daughter; Miss
Clara Ellis, a young Englishwoman, who remained
but a few years in this country, was the Gertrude;
Mrs. Dyott was Millinette, the French maid; and
Mrs. Edward Knight (Mary Ann Povey) played
Prudence, the maiden lady of a certain age. The part
of Adam Trueman, the blunt, old-fashioned, warm-
hearted farmer, with his unfashionable energy and
sturdy common-sense, pointing homely morals and
bursting social bubbles--"Seventy-two last August,
man! Strong as a hickory, and every whit as sound"-
-was for many years a favorite with the
representatives of "character old men" on our stage.
Mr. Blake, the original Adam in Philadelphia, was
particularly happy in the *rôle*, playing it many times
in New York; and E. L. Davenport made a decided
hit as Adam at the Olympic in London, in January,
1850, when the comedy was first produced in
England. Mr. Davenport on this occasion had the
support of his wife, who played Gertrude, and who
was then still billed as Miss Fanny Vining.

There is no record of Mrs. Mowatt's appearance in
Fashion, except on one evening in Philadelphia,
when she played Gertrude for the benefit of Mr.
Blake, and once in New York--at the Park, May 15,
1846. She felt that the character gave her no great
opportunity, and she never attempted it again.

Mrs. Mowatt's career as an actress was very
remarkable. She was one of the few persons of adult

years who, going upon the stage without the severe training and long apprenticeship so necessary even to indifferent dramatic success, display anything like brilliant dramatic qualities. She was an actress and a "star" born, not made. Her reasons for adopting the profession were as remarkable as the triumphs she won; her success as a playwright encouraging her, she said, to attempt to achieve like favor as a player. Every one familiar with the history of the theatre since it has had a history knows well how great is the distinction between producer and performer, and how few are the actors who have written clever plays, how few the authors who have become distinguished as actors upon the stage. The popularity of Miss Elizabeth Thompson's battle pictures would not encourage her to attempt to lead armies in the field; gun-makers are proverbially poor marksmen; and Von Bülow would never succeed were he to attempt the construction of a grand-piano.

Mrs. Mowatt, however, had stronger inducements than those given in her *Autobiography* for the step she took. In looking back upon her life, she felt that all of her tastes, studies, and pursuits from childhood had combined to make her an actress. She had exhibited a passion for theatrical entertainments when she was little more than an infant; she had written plays, such as they were, before she had seen the inside of a theatre, and she had played in an amateur way before she had ever seen a professional performance. Above and beyond all of these things she was a woman of uncommon intelligence and grace, almost a genius. She had, with some success, given public readings. She felt

the stage to be her destiny. She determined that her
destiny should be fulfilled, and she became a good
actress if not absolutely a great one, and seemingly
with little effort and few rebuffs. The pleasant
account she has given of her own theatrical
experiences, and her touching and beautiful defence
of those women who make their living on the stage,
have encouraged many ladies who have felt
themselves gifted with similar talents, and
possessed of like ambitions and aspirations, to make
the same attempts, and generally to fail.

There have been *débutantes* enough in New York
since the *début* of Mrs. Mowatt to fill to
overflowing the auditorium of any single city
theatre, could they be gathered under one roof to
witness the first effort of the next aspirant, whoever
she may be. During the season of 1876-77 alone,
not less than seven ladies--Mrs. Louise M.
Pomeroy, Miss Bessie Darling, Miss Anna
Dickinson, Mrs. J. H. Hackett, Miss Minnie
Cummings, Miss Marie Wainwright, and Miss
Adelaide Lennox--in leading parts made their first
bows to metropolitan audiences, without training or
experience; and the season was not considered a
particularly strong one in *débutantes* at that. For
much of this Mrs. Mowatt, unconsciously and
unwittingly, was responsible. Her sudden success
turned many heads, while the equally sudden
failures, not recorded, but very many in number,
have been quite forgotten, and will be still ignored
as long as there are new Camilles and new Juliets to
achieve greatness at one fell swoop, and as long as
there are unwise friends and speculative managers
to encourage them. The careers of these candidates

for dramatic fame, as they are familiar to the world, are certainly not inspiring to their foolish sisters who would follow them. A few still in the profession are filling, creditably but ingloriously, humble positions; a very small proportion have by the hardest of work become prominent and popular; but the great majority, dispirited and disheartened, have gone back to the private life from which they sprung, without song, without honor, and without tears, except the many tears they have shed themselves.

Mrs. Mowatt was never behind the scenes of a theatre until she was taken to witness a rehearsal of *Fashion* the day before its first production. Her second passage through a "stage door" was when she had her single rehearsal of *The Lady of Lyons*, in which she made her *début*, and she became an actress, and a triumphant one, three weeks after her determination to go upon the stage was formed. Her house was crowded, the applause was genuine and discriminating, and one gentleman, wholly unprejudiced and of great experience, publicly pronounced it "the best first appearance" he ever saw.

The performance took place at the Park Theatre, New York, on the 13th of June, 1845, less than three months after the production of her comedy. The occasion was the benefit of Mr. Crisp, who had given her the little instruction her limited time permitted her to receive, and who played Claude to her Pauline, Mrs. Vernon representing Madame Deschapelles. While she writes candidly in her *Autobiography* of her hopes, her experiences, and her trials, she modestly says but little of the decided praise from all quarters which she certainly received, the account of her success here given being taken from current journals and from the recollections of old theatre-goers, not from her own story of her theatrical life.

On the 13th of July of the same year (1845) Mrs. Mowatt appeared at Niblo's Garden, playing a very successful engagement of two weeks, supported by Messrs. Crisp, Chippendale, E. L. Davenport, Thomas Placide, Nickinson, John Sefton, and Mrs. Watts, afterwards Mrs. Sefton. Here she assumed her second *rôle*, that of Juliana in the *Honeymoon*, and more than strengthened the favorable impression she had made as Pauline.

During the first year she was upon the stage she acted more than two hundred nights, and in almost every important city in the United States, playing Lady Teazle, Mrs. Haller in *The Stranger*, Lucy Ashton in the *Bride of Lammermoor*, Katherine in the *Taming of the Shrew*, Julia, Juliet, and all of the then most popular characters in the line of juvenile tragedy and comedy. The amount of labor, physical and mental, she endured during this period must have been enormous; and the intellectual strain alone was enough to have destroyed the strongest mental constitution. In the history of the stage in all countries there is no single instance of a mere novice playing so many important parts so many nights, before so many different audiences, and winning so much and such merited praise, as did this lady during the first twelve months of her career as an actress.

Mrs. Mowatt went to England in the autumn of
1847, where her success was as marked as in her
own country, and more, perhaps, to her professional
credit. She had to contend with a certain prejudice
against her nationality, which still existed in
Britain; she was compared with the leading English
actresses of long experience in their own familiar
rôles, and she could not depend upon the social
popularity and personal good-will which were so
strongly in her favor at home. Her English *début*
was made in Manchester a few weeks after her
arrival. Her first appearance in London was at the
Princess's Theatre on the 5th of January, 1848; Mr.
Davenport, who had played opposite characters to
her during her American tours, giving her excellent
support during her English engagements. She
returned to America in the summer of 1851, greatly
improved in her personal appearance and in her art.
Her subsequent career here, as long as she remained
upon the stage, was marked with uniform success,
the reputation she had acquired on the other side of
the water establishing even more strongly her
claims on this.

Mrs. Mowatt, after nine years of experience as an
actress, took her farewell of the stage at Niblo's
Garden on the evening of the 3d of June, 1854. As
her *Autobiography* was published during the
preceding year her reason for this step is not given,
unless it was her marriage to Mr. Ritchie a few days
later. The occasion was very interesting. A
testimonial signed by many of the leading citizens,
and highly eulogistic, was presented to her, and her
last appearance created as great an excitement in the
dramatic and social world as did her first. The play

selected was *The Lady of Lyons*, the same in which she made her *début*. Old play-goers who still remember her consider her one of the most satisfactory Paulines who have been seen in this country, and the part was always a favorite of her own. On the last play-bill which contains her name are found as her support the names of Walter G. Keeble, who played Claude; of George H. Andrews, then a favorite "old man," who played Colonel Damas; of T. B. De Walden, who played Glavis; and of Mrs. Mann, who played Madame Deschapelles. Mrs. Mowatt never again appeared here, or elsewhere, in any public capacity.

Anna Cora Ogden was born in Bordeaux, France, during a visit of her parents to that country in 1819. She married James Mowatt, a young lawyer of New York, when she was only fifteen years of age. Her first appearance as a public reader was made in Boston in 1841--Mr. Mowatt's financial troubles leading her to seek that means of contributing to her own support. During this same year she gave readings in the hall of the old Stuyvesant Institute in New York. In 1845, as has been shown above, she became an actress. Mr. Mowatt died in London in the spring of 1851. On the 7th of June, 1854, she was married (on Staten Island) to William F. Ritchie, of the Richmond *Enquirer*, and she died in the little English village of Henley-on-the-Thames in the month of July, 1870, Mr. Ritchie surviving her some years, and dying in Lower Brandon, Virginia, on the 24th of April, 1877.

Mrs. Mowatt is described, by those who remember her in the first flush of her youth and her success, as "a fascinating actress and accomplished lady; in person fragile and exquisitely delicate, with a face in whose calm depths the beautiful and pure alone were mirrored, a voice ever soft, gentle, and low, a subdued earnestness of manner, a winning witchery of enunciation, and a grace and refinement in every action"; and it was felt by her admirers that she would have become, had she remained longer in the profession, a consummate artist--one of the greatest this country has ever produced.

After her retirement, and until the breaking out of the civil war, her home in Richmond, Virginia, was the centre of all that was refined and cultured in the Southern capital. She devoted herself to literature and to her social and family cares, writing during this period her *Mimic Life; or, Before and Behind the Curtain*, in which she spoke so many kind and encouraging words of her sisters in the profession, particularly of the ballet girls and the representatives of small and thankless parts, who contribute in their quiet way so much to the public amusement, and who too often, by authors and public, are entirely ignored. Among her more important works, other than those already mentioned here, written in her youth and later life, was *Gulzara; or, The Persian Slave*, a play without heroes, the scenes of which were laid within the walls of a Turkish harem, and which was chiefly remarkable from the fact that the only male character in the *dramatis personæ* was a boy of ten years.

Marion Harland, in her *Recollections of a Christian Actress*, printed a few years ago, has paid the

highest tribute to the personal worth of Mrs.
Mowatt. What she accomplished during her
professional life has, in a manner, been shown here.
She was a representative American woman of
whom American women have every reason to be
proud; and as the writer of the first absolutely
American society play, she must be forgiven the
harm her brilliant and easy success as an actress
has, by its example, since done to the American
stage.

Very few of our earlier native dramatists followed
the fashion set by Mrs. Mowatt in writing original
plays of American social life. "Plays of
contemporaneous society," as they were called,
were popular and fairly successful here; but they
were the charming home comedies of men like
Byron or Robertson, thoroughly English in
character and tone, or they were taken from the
French and the German, with purely foreign
incidents and scenes. Some of these were
"localized," and thus became cruel libels upon
American men and manners, except upon such
Americans as are influenced by the worship of *The
Mighty Dollar*, or such as are to be found only in
Our Boarding-houses, and *Under the Gas-light*.
The New York play-goer of thirty years since
looked in vain upon the stage for the domestic
stories of American city and country life which he
found in the then new novels of Theodore
Winthrop, or in the then familiar poems of Dr.
Holland. Until Joshua Whitcomb appeared we saw
no American Peter Probity in an American *Chimney
Corner*; and until Bronson Howard and David
Lloyd and Brander Matthews and Edgar Fawcett

began to write American plays we saw no American
Haversack in an American *Old Guard*--not even an
American Peter Teazle or an American John
Mildmay; while we could not help feeling that *Still
Waters Run as Deep* in this country as they run in
the old, and that the *School for Scandal* in real life
has as many graduates and undergraduates in the
United States as it has anywhere else.

If an American character was drawn at all, he was
too apt to be a Solon Shingle or a Mose; if an
American play was written at all, its scenes were
laid on *Sandy Bars*, or in the false and unhealthful
atmosphere of *Saratoga* or *Long Branch*. While
London managers presented *Orange Blossoms* and
Two Roses, the managers of New York and Boston
set *Diamonds* and *Pearls*. The English flowers were
fresh and fragrant; the American jewels, although
they had a certain sparkle, were too often paste. The
exotics flourished and bloomed on our soil for a
time, it is true; but if they had been native buds they
would have withered in a week, or else, like so
many other indigenous plants, have been left to
waste their sweetness in the pigeon-holes of
managers' desks. So strong was this unnatural
prejudice against the production of an American
picture of American home-life upon the American
stage, that in one of the brightest American
comedies ever taken from the French Mr. Hurlburt
was forced to go abroad with his characters, and to
place his *Americans in Paris*.

All this is not so true of the stage of to-day as it was
at the beginning of the second century of our
national drama. Scores of native writers, during the

past decade or two, have presented American plays which have been clean and clever, even if they have not yet become classic. But it is a striking fact that the first three original "society plays" which were in any way successful upon the American stage were from the pens of women--Mrs. Mowatt's *Fashion*, Mrs. Bateman's *Self*, and Miss Heron's *The Belle of the Season*--and that since their production the name of a woman has very rarely appeared upon the bills as the author of a play.

During the ten years which followed the first performance of *Fashion* it had a few rivals--comedies and dramas, satirical or otherwise--which treated, or pretended to treat, of that which asserts itself to be "the higher stratum of American society." Among the longer lived of these were *Extremes*, a local New York play, which ran for three weeks at the Broadway Theatre in 1850; a dramatization of Mr. Curtis's *Potiphar Papers*, brought out at Burton's Theatre in 1854, in which Charles Fisher made a great hit as Creamcheese; and Mr. De Walden's *Upper Ten and Lower Twenty*, also at Burton's, in 1854, in which Mr. Burton himself, as Christopher Crookpath, a serious part, was a genuine surprise to his audience, and created a profound impression. *Extremes*, by a Baltimore gentleman, was never repeated here; the version of Mr. Curtis's work--happily called *Our Best Society*--was merely an adaptation; Mr. De Walden was not a native writer; and only one of these productions, and that one the least successful, was an original American play.

"*Self*, an original New York comedy in three acts,"

by Mrs. H. L. Bateman, was seen for the first time in New York at Mr. Burton's Chambers Street house on the 27th of October, 1856. The plot was slight, and the play was long and a trifle dull. It was the story of a young girl (Mrs. E. L. Davenport) with a few thousands of dollars of her own, which both of her parents were determined to possess. She gave the money to her father (Charles Fisher); the mother (Mrs. Amelia Parker) instigated the son (A. Morton) to forge a check for the amount; the forgery was discovered; the girl, to save her mother and her brother, confessed the crime which she did not commit, and was turned out-of-doors in ignominy and disgrace, Mr. Burton, the traditional stage uncle, rescuing and righting her in the end. All of this was not new, was not cheerful, and, it is to be hoped, was not "society"; but it was received with great praise, and it took its place in popular favor by the side of Mrs. Mowatt's comedy. *Self* was frequently repeated in New York, notably at Wallack's Theatre, now the Star, in the Summer of 1869, when it introduced John E. Owens as Unit, and where it ran for three weeks, Miss Effie Germon playing the heroine, and playing it well. Mr. Owens made of Unit what is called a "star part." It gave him an opportunity for the display of his peculiar comedy powers, and he presented it with a variety and force of expression which was not always to be seen in his acting. In it he appealed more to the hearts of his audiences than in Solon Shingle; and, next to his Caleb Plummer, his Unit is the pleasantest and most perfect picture he has left in the memory of his friends.

Mrs. Bateman was the daughter of Joseph Cowell, a

well-known theatrical manager in the South and
West, who came to this country from England in
1821, and whose *Thirty Years Among the Players* is
known to all collectors of dramatic books. She went
upon the stage at New Orleans in 1837 or 1838, but
did not long remain an actress. She was successful
as a manager; and she was the author of *Geraldine*,
a tragedy, and of a dramatization of Longfellow's
Evangeline. For many years she was known only as
the mother of the Bateman Children.

At Winter Garden, on the evening of March 12,
1862, Miss Matilda Heron produced for the first
time *The Belle of the Season*, advertised as "a new
and original home play," and as written by Miss
Heron herself. Its scenes were laid in the parks of
Niagara and in Fifth Avenue drawing-rooms, but it
suggested too many familiar plays of *The Lady of
Lyons* school to be altogether free from the
suspicion of imitation. That it came from Miss
Heron's own brain and pen, however, there could be
little doubt; it had, as a literary effort, many of the
faults and virtues and strong characteristics so
curiously blended in the acting of its author. The
production, as a whole, was what is termed
"emotional," the part of the heroine being peculiarly
so. Unquestionably Miss Heron wrote it to fit
herself, and unquestionably it did not fit her so well
as did Camille, upon which so much of her fame as
an actress now rests. She had all of an author's
fondness for the part and for the play. She
considered both her greatest works. She produced
the comedy many times in many cities of the Union,
not always to the benefit of her purse or of her
professional reputation, and when urged by her

business manager to withdraw it altogether, she is said to have replied, with characteristic determination, that *The Belle of the Season* she wanted to play, *The Belle of the Season* she would play, and that when she died she wished nothing placed over her grave but the epitaph, "Here lies *The Belle of the Season*!"

Matilda Heron was one of the most remarkable actresses our stage has ever produced. With an intensity and passion in her performances which, at times, were magnificent and carried everything before them, she displayed professional shortcomings and infirmities which were often glaring and unpardonable; but she made and held, by the force of her own genius--and genius she certainly possessed--a position which few modern actresses have ever reached. Her personal faults were of the head rather than of the heart, and may they now rest lightly on her!

Miss Heron's immediate successors as native playwrights of society dramas were Miss Olive Logan, with *Surf; or, Summer Scenes at Long Branch*, at Daly's Theatre in 1870; Bronson Howard, with *Saratoga* in 1870-71, with *Diamonds* in 1873, and with *Moorcroft* in 1874; James Steele Mackaye, with *Marriage* in 1873; and Andrew C. Wheeler, with *Twins*, and Mr. Marsden, with *Clouds*, in 1876.

Anything like an enumeration of the original American society plays written and produced here during the last ten or fifteen years is not possible within the limits of a single chapter. They have been very many, and of all degrees of merit, the best and most creditable perhaps being *Young Mrs. Winthrop*, *Old Love Letters*, *A Gold Mine*, *Esmeralda*, *Conscience*, and *The Charity Ball*; but how long these are to live, and how they are to be regarded by the next generation--if the next generation has ever a chance to regard them at all-- of course remains to be seen. *Fashion*, the first of the lot, survives only in its printed form, and the shell of the locust gives but a faint dry rattle, while the locust itself is as much alive as when *The School for Scandal* was first seen in America over a century ago. Have we a Sheridan among us? or is he still twenty years away?

ACT II.

THE AMERICAN STAGE NEGRO.

Bottom: "I have a reasonable good ear in music:
let's have the tongs and the bones."--*Midsummer
Night's Dream*, Act iv. Sc. 1.

Shakspere's Moor of Venice was one of the earliest
of the stage negroes, as he is one of the best. If the
Account of the Revels be not a forgery, he appeared
before the court of the first English James in 1604,
and he certainly was seen at the Globe Theatre, on
the Bankside, on the 30th of April, 1610. Othello is
hardly the typical African of the modern drama,
although Roderigo speaks of him as having thick
lips, and notwithstanding the fact that he himself is
made to regret, in the third act of the tragedy, that
he is "black, and has not those soft parts of
conversation that chamberers have." Shakspere
unquestionably believed that the Moors were
negroes; and as he made Verges and Dogberry
cockney watchmen, and altered history, geography,
and chronology to suit himself and the requirements
of the stage, so he meant to invest his Moorish hero
with all of the personal attributes, as well as with all
of the moral characteristics, of the negroes as they
were known to Englishmen in Shakspere's day.

Othello was followed, in 1696, by *Oroonoko*, a
tragedy in five acts, by Thomas Southerne. The real
Oroonoko was an African prince stolen from his
native kingdom of Angola during the reign of
Charles the Second, and sold as a slave in an
English settlement in the West Indies. Aphra Behn

saw and became intimate with him at Surinam, when her father was Lieutenant-General of the islands, and made him the hero of the tale upon which the dramatist based his once famous play. With the more humble slaves by whom he was surrounded, the stage Oroonoko spoke in the stilted blank-verse of the dramatic literature of that period, and without any of the accent or phraseology of the original West Indian blacks. Mr. Pope was the creator of Oroonoko; and the part was a favorite one of the elder Kean in England and of the elder Booth in this country. It has not been seen upon either stage in many years. Oroonoko, of course, had a black skin and woolly hair. When Jack Bannister, who began his career as a tragic actor, said to Garrick that he proposed to attempt the hero of Southerne's drama, he was told by the great little man that, in view of his extraordinarily thin person, he would "look as much like the character as a chimney-sweep in consumption!" It was to Bannister, on this same occasion, that Garrick uttered the well-known aphorism, "Comedy is a very serious thing!"

Mungo was a stage negro of a very different stamp, and the first of his race. He figured in *The Padlock*, a comic opera, words by Isaac Bickerstaffe, music by Charles Dibdin, first presented at Drury Lane in 1768. Mungo was the slave of Don Diego, a West Indian planter. It was written for and at the suggestion of John Moody, who had been in Barbadoes, where he had studied the dialect and the manners of the blacks. He never played the part, however, which was originally assumed by Dibdin himself. Mungo sang:

"Dear heart, what a terrible life I am led! A dog has a better that's sheltered and fed. Night and day 'tis the same; My pain is deir game; Me wish to de Lord me was dead! Whate'er's to be done Poor black must run. Mungo here, Mungo dere, Mungo everywhere; Above and below, Sirrah, come, sirrah, go; Do so, and do so. Oh! oh! Me wish to de Lord me was dead!"

This is a style of ballad which has been very popular with Mungo's descendants ever since. It may be added that Mungo got drunk in the second act, and was very profane throughout.

The great and original Mungo in America was Lewis Hallam, the younger, who first played the part in New York, and for his own benefit, on the 29th of May, 1769, at the theatre in John Street. Dunlap says, "In *The Padlock* Mr. Hallam was unrivalled to his death, giving Mungo with a truth derived from the study of the negro slave character which Dibdin, the writer, could not have conceived." Mungo is never seen in the present time. Ira Aldridge, the negro tragedian, played Othello and Mungo occasionally on the same night in his natural skin; but Mungo may be said to have virtually died with Hallam, and to have gone to meet Oroonoko in that land of total oblivion to which Othello is destined to be a stranger for many years to come.

In 1781 a pantomime entitled *Robinson Crusoe* was presented at Drury Lane. It was believed by the editor of the *Biographia Dramatica* to have been "contrived by Mr. Sheridan, whose powers, if it really be his performance, do not seem adapted to the production of such kind of entertainments. The scenery, by Loutherbourg, has a very pleasing effect, but, considered in every other light, it is a truly insipid exhibition." Friday, in coffee-colored tights and blackened face, was naturally a prominent figure. The pantomime was produced at the Theatre Royal, Bath, during the next year, when Mr. Henry Siddons appeared as one of the savages. This gentleman, who played Othello on the same boards a few seasons later, is only remembered now as having given his name to the greatest actress who ever spoke the English tongue. This same *Robinson Crusoe and Harlequin Friday* was seen at the John Street Theatre, New York, on the 11th of January, 1786; while at the Park Theatre on the 11th of September, 1817, Mr. Bancker played Friday in *The Bold Buccaneers; or, The Discovery of Robinson Crusoe*, a melodrama which was very popular in its day.

Charles C. Moreau, of New York, possesses a very curious and almost unique bill of "The African Company," at "The Theatre in Mercer Street, in the rear of the 1 Mile Stone, Broadway." *Tom and Jerry* was presented by a number of gentlemen and ladies entirely unknown to dramatic fame, and the performance concluded with the pantomime of *Obi: or, Three Finger'd Jack*. Unfortunately the bill is not dated. Mr. Ireland believes this to have been a company of negro amateurs who played in New York about 1820 or 1821, but who have left no other mark upon the history of the stage; and the historians know nothing of the "theatre" they occupied. Broadway at Prince Street is one mile from the City Hall, although the stone recording this fact has long since disappeared.

A number of stage negroes will be remembered by habitual theatre-goers, and students of the drama-- two very different things, by-the-way, for the man who sees plays rarely reads them, and *vice versa*: Zeke, in Mrs. Mowatt's *Fashion*; Pete, in *The Octoroon*; Uncle Tom; Topsy, whom Charles Reade called "idiopathic"; a cleverly conceived character in Bronson Howard's *Moorcraft*; and the delightful band of "Full Moons," led for many seasons by "Johnny" Wild at Harrigan and Hart's Theatre, who were so absolutely true to the life of Thompson Street and South Fifth Avenue.

In the absence of anything like a complete and satisfactory history of negro minstrelsy, it is not possible to discover its genesis, although it is the only branch of the dramatic art, if properly it can claim to be an art at all, which has had its origin in this country, while the melody it has inspired is certainly our only approach to a national music. Scattered throughout the theatrical literature of the early part of the century are to be found many different accounts of the rise and progress of the African on the stage, each author having his own particular "father of negro song." Charles White, an old Ethiopian comedian and manager, gives the credit to Gottlieb Graupner, who appeared in Boston in 1799, basing his statement upon a copy of Russell's *Boston Gazette* of the 30th of December of that year, which contains an advertisement of a performance to be given on the date of publication at the Federal Street Theatre. At the end of the

second act of *Oroonoko*, according to Mr. White,
Mr. Graupner, in character, sang "The Gay Negro
Boy," accompanying the air with the banjo; and
although the house was draped in mourning for
General Washington, such was the enthusiasm of
the audience that the performer had to bring his
little bench from the wings again and again to sing
his song. W. W. Clapp, Jr., in his *History of the
Boston Stage*, says that the news of the death of
Washington was received in that city on the 24th of
December, and that the theatre remained "closed for
a week;" and was reopened with "A Monody," in
which "Mrs. Barrett, in the character of the Genius
of America, appeared weeping over the Tomb of
her Beloved Hero"; but there is no mention, then or
later, of Mr. Graupner or of "The Gay Negro Boy."

Mr. White says further that "the next popular negro
song was 'The Battle of Plattsburg,' sung by an actor
vulgarly known as 'Pig-Pie Herbert,' at a theatre in
Albany, in 1815"; but H. D. Stone, in a volume
called *The Drama*, published in Albany in 1873,
credits "a member of the theatrical company of the
name of Hop Robinson" as the singer of the song;
while "Sol" Smith, an eye-witness of this
performance, gives still another and very different
account of it. According to Smith's *Autobiography*
published by Messrs. Harper and Brothers in 1868,
Andrew Jackson Allen produced at the Green Street
Theatre in Albany, in 1815, a drama called *The
Battle of Lake Champlain*, the action taking place
on real ships floating in real water. "In this piece,"
says Smith, "Allen played the character of a negro,
and sang a song of many verses (being the first
negro song, I verily believe, ever heard on the

American stage)." Two verses of this ballad, quoted by Smith "from memory," will give a very fair idea of its claims to popularity:

"Backside Albany stan' Lake Champlain-- Little pond half full of water; Plat-te-burg dar too, close 'pon de main: Town small; he grow big, dough, herea'ter.

"On Lake Champlain Uncle Sam set he boat, An' Massa Macdonough he sail 'em; While General Macomb make Plat-te-burg he home, Wid de army whose courage nebber fail 'em."

Andrew Allen was a very quaint character, and he deserves a paragraph to himself. Born in the city of New York in 1776, he appeared, according to his own statement, as a page in *Romeo and Juliet* at the theatre in John Street in 1786, on the strength of which, as the oldest living actor, he assumed for years before his death the title of "Father of the American Stage." He was more famous as a cook than as a player, however, and he is the subject of innumerable theatrical anecdotes, none of which are greatly to his credit. He was called "Dummy Allen" because he was very deaf and exceedingly loquacious; he adored the hero of New Orleans, whose name he appropriated when Jackson was elected President of the United States; and he was devoted to Edwin Forrest, whose costumer, dresser, and personal slave he was for many years. He invented and patented a silver leather much used in the decoration of stage dresses; and he kept a restaurant in Dean Street, Albany, and later a similar establishment near the Bowery Theatre,

New York, being a very familiar figure in the streets of both cities. Mr. Phelps, in his *Players of a Century* (Albany, New York, 1880), describes him in his later years as tall and erect in person, with firmly compressed features, an eye like a hawk's, nose slightly Romanesque, and hair mottled gray. He wore a fuzzy white hat, a coat of blue with bright brass buttons, and carried a knobby cane. He spoke in a sharp, decisive manner, often giving wrong answers, and invariably mistaking the drift of the person with whom he was conversing. He died in New York in 1853, and Mr. Phelps preserves the inscription upon his monument at Cypress Hills Cemetery, which was evidently his own composition: "From his cradle he was a scholar; exceedingly wise, fair-spoken, and persuading; lofty and sour to them that loved him not, but to those men that sought him sweet as summer."

Apropos of Allen's association with Edwin Forrest, and of Smith's assertion that Allen sang the first negro song ever sung on the American stage, it may not be out of place here to quote W. R. Alger's *Life of Forrest*. Speaking of Forrest's early and checkered experiences as a strolling player in the far West, Mr. Alger says that perhaps the most surprising fact connected with this portion of his career is "that he was the first actor who ever represented on the stage the Southern plantation negro with all his peculiarities of dress, gait, accent, dialect, and manner." In 1823, at the Globe Theatre, Cincinnati, Ohio, under the management of "Sol" Smith, Forrest did play a negro in a farce by Smith, called *The Tailor in Distress*, singing and dancing, and winning the compliment from a veritable black in his audience that he was "nigger all ober!" Lawrence Barrett, in his *Life of Forrest*, quotes the bill of this evening, which shows Forrest as a modern dandy in the first play, as Cuffee, a Kentucky negro, in the second, and as Sancho Panza in the pantomime of *Don Quixote*, which closed the evening's entertainment.

Forrest was by no means the only eminent American actor who hid his light behind a black mask. "Sol" Smith himself relates how he became a supernumerary at the Green Street Theatre, in Albany, in his fourteenth year, playing one of the blood-thirsty associates of *Three-fingered Jack* with a preternaturally smutty face, which he forgot to wash one eventful night, to the astonishment of his own family, who forced him to retire for a time to private life.

At Vauxhall Garden, in the Bowery, a little south of and nearly opposite the site of Cooper Institute, a young lad named Bernard Flaherty, born in Cork, Ireland, is said to have sung negro songs and to have danced negro dances in 1838 to help support a widowed mother, who lived to see him carried to an honored grave in 1876, mourned by the theatre-going population of the whole country. In 1840, as Barney Williams, he made a palpable hit in the character of Pat Rooney, in *The Omnibus*, at the Franklin Theatre, New York. He certainly played "darky parts," such as they were, for a number of years before and after that date; and he is perhaps the one man upon the American stage with whom anything like negro minstrelsy will never be associated, not so much because of his high rank in his profession as on account of the Hibernian style of his later-day performances, and of the strong accent which always clung to him, and which suggested his native city rather than the cork he used to burn to color his face.

In 1850, when Edwin Booth was seventeen, and a year after his *début* as Tressel at the Boston Museum, he gave an entertainment with John S. Clarke, a youth of the same age, at the court-house in Belair, Maryland. They read selections from *Richelieu* and *The Stranger*, as well as the quarrel scene from *Julius Cæsar*, singing during the evening (with blackened faces) a number of negro melodies, "using appropriate dialogue"--as Mrs. Asia Booth Clarke records in the memoir of her brother--"and accompanying their vocal attempts with the somewhat inharmonious banjo and bones." Mrs. Clarke reprints the programme of this performance, and pictures the distress of the young tragedians when they discovered, on arriving in the town, that the simon-pure negro they had employed as an advance agent had in every instance posted their bills upsidedown.

Mr. Booth, during his first San Francisco engagement, appeared more than once in the character of what was then termed a "Dandy Nigger;" and he remembers that his father, "some time in the forties," played Sam Johnson in *Bone Squash* at the Front Street Theatre, Baltimore, for the benefit of an old theatrical acquaintance, and played it with great applause. Lawrence Barrett's negro parts, in the beginning of his career, were

George Harris and Uncle Tom himself, in a
dramatization of Mrs. Stowe's famous tale.

Among the stage negroes of later years, whom the
world is not accustomed to associate with that
profession, Ralph Keeler is one of the most
prominent. His "Three Years a Negro Minstrel,"
first published in the *Atlantic Monthly* for July,
1869, and afterwards elaborated in his *Vagabond
Adventures*, is very entertaining and instructive
reading, and gives an excellent idea of the
wandering minstrel life of that period. He began his
career at Toledo, Ohio, when he was not more than
eleven years of age; and under the management of
the celebrated Mr. Booker, the subject of the once
famous song, "Meet Johnny Booker on the
Bowling-green," he "danced 'Juba'" in small canton-
flannel knee-breeches (familiarly known as pants)
cheap lace, tarnished gold tinsel, a corked face, and
a woolly wig, to the great gratification of the
Toledans, who for several months, with pardonable
pride, hailed him as their own particular infant
phenomenon. At the close of his first engagement
he received what was termed a "rousing benefit,"
the entire proceeds of which, as was the custom of
the time, going into the pockets of his enterprising
managers. During his short although distinguished
professional life he was associated with such artists
as "Frank" Lynch, "Mike" Mitchell, "Dave" Reed,
and "Professor" Lowe, the balloonist, and he was
even offered a position in E. P. Christy's company
in New York--the highest compliment which could
then be paid to budding talent. Keeler, a brilliant
but eccentric writer, whose *Vagabond Adventures* is
too good, in its way, to be forgotten so soon, was a

man of decided mark as a journalist. He went to
Cuba in 1873 as special correspondent of the New
York *Tribune*, and suddenly and absolutely
disappeared. He is supposed to have been murdered
and thrown into the sea.

Lynch, when Keeler first knew him, had declined
into the fat and slippered end man, too gross to
dance, who ordinarily played the tambourine and
the banjo, but who could, and not infrequently did,
perform everything in the orchestra, from a solo on
the penny trumpet to an obligato on the double-
bass. He had been associated as a boy, in 1839 or
1840, under Barnum's management, with "Jack"
Diamond, who was "the best representative of
Ethiopian break-downs" in his day, and, according
to P. T. Barnum, the prototype of the many
performers of that sort who have entertained the
public ever since. Lynch asserted that he and
Barnum had appeared together in black faces; and
Mr. Barnum, in his *Autobiography*, called Mr.
Lynch "an orphan vagabond" whom he had picked
up on the road; neither statement seeming to be
entirely true. Lynch was his own worst enemy, and,
like so many of his kind, he died in poverty and
obscurity, his most perfect "break-down" being his
own!

It is a melancholy fact that George Holland joined
Christy and Wood's minstrels in 1857, playing
female characters in a blackened face, and dividing
with George Christy the honors of a short season.
He returned to Wallack's Theatre in 1858. This is a
page in dramatic history which old play-goers do
not like to read.

The name of John B. Gough, the temperance orator, occurs occasionally in the reminiscences of old minstrels. He certainly did appear upon the stage as a comic singer in New York and elsewhere during his early and dissipated youth, and even gave exhibitions of ventriloquism and the like in low bar-rooms for the sake of the few pennies he could gather to keep himself in liquor, as he himself describes; but there is no hint in his *Autobiography* of his ever having appeared in a blackened face, and his theatrical life, if it may be so called, was very short.

Joseph Jefferson, the third and present bearer of that honored name, was unquestionably the youngest actor who ever made his mark with a piece of burnt cork. The story of his first appearance is told by William Winter in his volume entitled *The Jeffersons*. Coming from a family of actors, the boy, as was natural, was reared amid theatrical surroundings, and when only four years of age--in 1833--he was brought upon the stage by Thomas D. Rice himself, on a benefit occasion at the Washington Theatre. Little Joe, blackened and arrayed precisely like his senior, was carried onto the stage in a bag upon the shoulders of the shambling Ethiopian, and emptied from it with the appropriate couplet,

"Ladies and gentlemen, I'd have you for to know I's got a little darky here to jump Jim Crow."

Mrs. John Drew, who was present, says that the boy instantly assumed the exact attitude of Jim Crow Rice, and sang and danced in imitation of his sable companion, a perfect miniature likeness of that long, ungainly, grotesque, and exceedingly droll comedian.

Thomas D. Rice is generally conceded to have been the founder of Ethiopian minstrelsy. Although, as has been seen, it did not originate with him, he made it popular on both sides of the Atlantic, and his image deserves an honored niche in its cathedral. The history of "Jim Crow" Rice, as he was affectionately called for many years, has been written by many scribes and in many different ways, the most complete and most truthful account, perhaps, being that of Edmon S. Conner, who described in the columns of the New York *Times*, June 5, 1881, what he saw and remembered of the birth of Jim Crow. Mr. Conner was a member of the company at the Columbia Street Theatre, Cincinnati, in 1828-29, when he first met Rice, "doing little negro bits" between the acts at that house, notably a sketch he had studied from life in Louisville the preceding summer. Back of the Louisville theatre was a livery-stable kept by a man named Crow. The actors could look into the stable-yard from the windows of their dressing-rooms, and were fond of watching the movements of an old and decrepit slave who was employed by the proprietor to do all sorts of odd jobs. As was the custom among the negroes, he had assumed his master's name, and called himself Jim Crow. He was very much deformed--the right shoulder was drawn up high, and the left leg was stiff and crooked at the knee, which gave him a painful but at the same time ludicrous limp. He was in the habit of crooning a queer old tune, to which he had applied words of his own. At the end of each verse he gave a peculiar step, "rocking de heel" in the manner since so general among the many generations of his imitators; and these were the words of his refrain:

"Wheel about, turn about, Do jis so, An' ebery time I wheel about I jump Jim Crow."

Rice closely watched this unconscious performer, and recognized in him a character entirely new to the stage. He wrote a number of verses, quickened and slightly changed the air, made up exactly like the original, and appeared before a Louisville audience, which, as Mr. Conner says, "went mad with delight," recalling him on the first night at least twenty times. And so Jim Crow jumped into fame and something that looks almost like immortality. "Sol" Smith says that the character was first seen in a piece by Solon Robinson, called *The Rifle*, and that he, Smith, "helped Rice a little in fixing the tune."

Other cities besides Louisville claim Jim Crow. Francis Courtney Wemyss, in his *Autobiography*, says he was a native of Pittsburg, whose name was Jim Cuff; while Robert P. Nevin, in the *Atlantic Monthly* for November, 1867, declares that the original was a negro stage-driver of Cincinnati, and that Pittsburg was the scene of Rice's first appearance in the part--a local negro there, whose professional career was confined to holding his mouth open for pennies thrown to him on the docks and the streets, furnishing the wardrobe for the initial performance.

Rice was born in the Seventh Ward of New York in
1808. He was a supernumerary at the Park Theatre,
where "Sam" Cowell remembered him in
Bombastes Furioso attracting so much attention by
his eccentricities that Hilson and Barnes, the
leading characters in the cast, made a formal
complaint, and had him dismissed from the
company Cowell; adding that this man, whose name
did not even appear in the bills, was the only actor
on the stage whom the audience seemed to notice.
Cowell also describes him in Cincinnati, in 1829, as
a very unassuming modest young man, who wore "a
very queer hat, very much pointed down before and
behind, and very much cocked on one side." He
went to England in 1836, where he met with great
success, laid the foundation of a very comfortable
fortune, and professionally he was the Buffalo Bill
of the London of half a century ago. Mr. Ireland,
speaking of his popularity in this country, says that
he drew more money to the Bowery Theatre than
any other performer in the same period of time.

Rice was the author of many of his own farces,
notably *Bone Squash* and *The Virginia Mummy*, and
he was the veritable originator of the *genus* known
to the stage as the "dandy darky," represented
particularly in his creations of "Dandy Jim of
Caroline" and "Spruce Pink." He died in 1860,
never having forfeited the respect of the public or
the good-will of his fellow-men.

There were many lithographed and a few engraved
portraits of Rice made during the years of his great
popularity, a number of which are still preserved. In
Mr. McKee's collection he is to be seen dancing

"Jim Crow" in English as well as in American prints--as "Gumbo Chaff," on a flat-boat, and, in character, singing the songs "A Long Time Ago" and "Such a Gettin' Up-stairs." In the same collection, among prints of George Dimond and other half-remembered clog-dancers and singers, is a portrait of John N. Smith as "Jim Along Josey," on a sheet of music published by Firth & Hall in 1840; and, more curious and rare than any of these, upon a musical composition, "on which copyright was secured according to law October 7, 1824," is a picture of Mr. Roberts singing "Massa George Washington and Massa Lafayette" in a Continental uniform and with a blackened face. This would make James Roberts, a Scottish vocalist, who died in 1833, the senior of Jim Crow by a number of years.

George Washington Dixon, whose very name is now almost forgotten, also preceded Rice in this class of entertainment, but without Rice's talent, and with nothing like Rice's success. He sang "Coal Black Rose" and "The Long-tailed Blue" at the old amphitheatre in North Pearl Street, Albany, as early as 1827, and he claimed to have been the author of "Old Zip Coon," which he sang for Allen's benefit in Philadelphia in 1834. He became notorious as a "filibuster" at the time of the troubles in Yucatan, and he made himself particularly offensive to a large portion of the community as the editor of a scurrilous paper called the *Polyanthus*, published in New York. He was caned, shot at, imprisoned for libel, and finally forced to leave the city. He died in the Charity Hospital, New Orleans, in 1861.

Mr. White says that in early days negro songs were sung from the backs of horses in the sawdust ring; that Robert Farrell, "a circus actor," was the original "Zip Coon," and that the first colored gentleman to wear "The Long-tailed Blue" was Barney Burns, who broke his neck on a vaulting board in Cincinnati in 1838. When the historians disagree in this confusing way, who can possibly decide?

Rice very naturally had many imitators, and Jim Crow wheeled about the country with considerable success, particularly when the original was in other lands. In the collection of Mr. Moreau is a bill of "The Theatre" (the Park), dated May 4, 1833, in which Mr. Blakeley was announced to sing the "Comic Extravaganza of Jim Crow" between the comedy of *Laugh When You Can*, in which he played Costly, and the melodrama of *The Floating Beacon*, and preceded by "Signora Adelaide Ferrero in a new ballet dance entitled 'The Festival of Bacchus';" the entertainments in those days being varied and long. Thomas H. Blakeley was a popular representative of what are called "second old men," Mr. Ireland pronouncing him the best Sulky, Rowley, and Humphrey Dobbin ever seen on the New York stage: and the fact that such a man should have appeared at a leading theatre, between the acts, in plantation dress and with blackened face, shows better than anything else, perhaps, the respectable position held by the negro minstrel half a century ago.

Mr. White, so frequently quoted here, is an old minstrel who was part and parcel of what he has more than once described in the public press, and upon his authority the following account of the first *band* of negro minstrels is given. It was organized in the boarding-house of a Mrs. Brooks, in Catherine Street, New York, late in the winter of 1842, and it consisted of "Dan" Emmett, "Frank" Brower, "Billy" Whitlock, and "Dick" Pelham--the name of the really great negro minstrel being always shortened in this familiar way. According to Mr. White, they made their first appearance in public, for Pelham's benefit, at the Chatham Theatre, New York, on the 17th of February, 1843; later they went to other cities, and even to Europe. This statement was verified by a fragment of autobiography of William Whitlock, given to the New York *Clipper* by his daughter, Mrs. Edwin Adams, at the time of Whitlock's death. It is worth quoting here in full, although it contains no dates: "The organization of the minstrels I claim to be my own idea, and it cannot be blotted out. One day I asked Dan Emmett, who was in New York at the time, to practise the fiddle and the banjo with me at his boarding-house in Catherine Street. We went down there, and when we had practised Frank Brower called in by accident. He listened to our music, charmed to his soul[!]. I told him to join with the bones, which he did. Presently Dick Pelham came in, also by accident, and looked amazed. I asked him to procure a tambourine, and make one of the party, and he went out and got one. After practising for a while we went to the old resort of the circus crowd--the 'Branch,' in the Bowery--with our instruments, and in Bartlett's billiard-room performed for the first time as the Virginia Minstrels. A programme was made out, and the first time we appeared upon the stage before an audience was for the benefit of Pelham at the Chatham Theatre. The house was crammed and jammed with our friends; and Dick, of course, put ducats in his purse."

Emmett, describing this scene, places the time "in the spring of 1843," and says that they were all of them "end men, and all interlocutors." They sang songs, played their instruments, danced jigs, singly and doubly, and "did 'The Essence of Old Virginia' and the 'Lucy Long Walk Around.'" Emmett remained upon the minstrel stage for many years; he was a member of the Bryant troupe from 1858 to 1865, and he was the composer of many popular songs, including "Old Dan Tucker," "Boatman's Dance," "Walk Along, John," "Early in the Mornin'," and, according to some authorities, he was the author of "Dixie," which afterwards became the war-song of the South.

Mr. White, according to a biographical sketch published in the New York *Clipper*, was born in 1821. He played the accordion--when he was too young to be held responsible for the offence--at Thalian Hall, in Grand Street, New York, as long ago as 1843, and the next year organized what he called "'The Kitchen Minstrels' on the second floor of the corner of Broadway and Chambers Street. The first floor was occupied by Tiffany, Young & Ellis, jewellers; the third by the renowned Ottignon as a gymnasium. Here, where the venerable Palmo had introduced to delighted audiences the Italian opera, and regaled them with fragrant Mocha coffee handed around by obsequious waiters, he first came most prominently before the public.... In 1846 he opened the Melodeon at 53 Bowery." Here, as usual, there is a decided confusion of dates and of facts. *Valentine's Manual* for 1865 says, "Palmo's café, on the corner of Reade Street and Broadway, was a popular resort from 1835 to 1840, at which later period he abandoned his former occupation and erected the opera-house in Chambers Street, afterwards Burton's Theatre." Joseph N. Ireland, in his *Records of the New York Stage*, published in 1867, says--and Mr. Ireland is usually correct--"The fourth attempt to introduce the Italian opera in New York, and the second to give it an individual local habitation, was this season [1843-44], made by Ferdinand Palmo, on the site long previously occupied by Stoppani's Arcade Baths, in Chambers Street (Nos. 39 and 41), and nearly opposite the centre of the building on the north end of the Park originally erected for the city almshouse, and afterwards used for various public offices.... Signor Palmo had been a popular and successful *restaurateur* in Broadway between the hospital and Duane Street.... Palmo's Opera-house was first opened by its proprietor on the 3d of February, 1844"; while Charles T. Cook, of Tiffany & Co., who has been connected with that house for over forty years, shows by its records that Tiffany, Young & Ellis did not move to 271 Broadway, on the southwest corner of Chambers Street, until 1847, when they occupied the second floor as well as the first. That Sir Walter Raleigh, losing all confidence in the infallibility of human testimony, should have thrown the second part of his *History of the World* into the flames is not to be wondered at!

Mr. White, nevertheless, was prominently before the public for many years as manager and performer; he was associated with the "Virginia Serenaders," with "The Ethiopian Operatic Brothers" (Operatic Brother Barney Williams playing the tambourine at one end of the line); with "The Sable Sisters and Ethiopian Minstrels;" with "The New York Minstrels," etc. He introduced "Dan" Bryant to the public, and has done other good services in contributing to the healthful, harmless amusement of his fellow-men.

"Christy's Minstrels, organized in 1842," was the legend for a number of years upon the bills and advertisements of the company of E. P. Christy. This would give it precedence of the "Virginia Minstrels" by a few months at least. When the matter was called to the attention of Mr. Emmett, many years later, he wrote from Chicago on the 1st of May, 1877, that after his own band had gone to Europe a number of similar entertainments were given in all parts of the country, and that Enam Dickinson, who had had some experience in that line in other companies, had trained Christy's troupe in Buffalo in all the business of the scenes, Mr. Emmett believing that Mr. Christy simply claimed, and with truth, that he was "the first to harmonize and originate the present style of negro minstrelsy," meaning the singing in concert and the introduction of the various acts, which were universally followed by other bands on both sides of the Atlantic, and which have led our English brethren to give to all Ethiopian entertainments the generic name of "Christy Minstrels," as they call all top-boots "Wellingtons" and all policemen "Bobbies."

Christy's Minstrels proper began their metropolitan career at the hall of the Mechanics' Society, 472 Broadway, near Grand Street, early in 1846, and remained there until the summer of 1854, when Edwin P. Christy, the leader and founder of the company, retired from business. George Christy, who the year before had joined forces with Henry Wood at 444 Broadway, formerly Mitchell's Olympic, took both halls after the abdication of the elder Christy, and rattled the bones at one establishment, "Billy" Birch, afterwards so popular in San Francisco and New York, cutting similar capers at the other, and each performer appearing at both houses on the same evening.

Edwin P. Christy died in May, 1862. George Harrington, known to the stage as George Christy, died in May, 1868; while in April of the latter year Mechanics' Hall, with which in the minds of so many old New-Yorkers they are both so pleasantly associated, was entirely destroyed by fire, never to be rebuilt for minstrel uses.

The contemporaries and successors of the Christys were numerous and various. The air was full of their music, and dozens of halls in the city of New York alone echoed the patter of their clogged feet for years. Among the more famous of them the following may briefly be mentioned: Buckley's "New Orleans Serenaders" were organized in 1843; they consisted of George Swayne, Frederick, and R. Bishop Buckley, and were very popular throughout the country. "White's Serenaders" were at the Melodeon, 53 Bowery, perhaps as early as 1846, and certainly at White's Athenæum, 585 Broadway,

opposite the Metropolitan Hotel, as late as 1872.
The Harrington Minstrels were at Palmo's Opera-
house in 1847 or 1848. Bryant's Minstrels, as their
old play-bills show, were organized in 1857, when
they occupied Mechanics' Hall; they went to the
Tammany Building on Fourteenth Street in 1868,
were at 730 Broadway the next year, and opened the
hall on Twenty-third Street near Sixth Avenue in
1870, where they remained until Dan Bryant, the
last of his race, died in 1875. Wood's Minstrels
were at 514 Broadway, opposite the St. Nicholas
Hotel, in 1862 and later. "Sam" Sharpley's Minstrels
were at 201 Bowery in 1864. "Tony" Pastor's troupe
were in the same building in 1865, where they
remained two years; they were upon the site of the
Metropolitan Theatre--later Winter Garden--for a
few seasons, and until they removed to their present
cosey home near Tammany Hall. The San Francisco
Minstrels were at 585 Broadway in 1865, and in
1874 went to the more familiar hall on Broadway,
opposite the Sturtevant House, Budworth's
Minstrels opened the Fifth Avenue Hall, where the
Madison Square Theatre now stands, in 1866. Kelly
and Leon, who were on Broadway on the site of
Hope Chapel in 1867, where they were credited
with having "Africanized opéra bouffe," followed
Budworth to the Twenty-fourth Street house.
Besides these were the companies of Morris
Brothers, of Cotton and Murphy and Cotton and
Reed, of Hooley, of Haverly, of Dockstader, of
Pelham, of Pierce, of Campbell, of Pell and
Trowbridge, of Thatcher, Primrose and West, of
Huntley, and of very many more, to say nothing of
the bands of veritable negroes who have endeavored
to imitate themselves in imitation of their white

brethren in all parts of the land. Brander Matthews, in an article on "Negro Minstrelsy," printed in the London *Saturday Review* in 1884, and afterwards published as one of the chapters of a volume of *Saturday Review* essays, entitled *The New Book of Sports* (London, 1885), describes a "minstrel show" given by the negro waiters of one of the large summer hotels in Saratoga a few summers before, in which, "when the curtains were drawn aside, discovering a row of sable performers, it was perceived, to the great and abiding joy of the spectators, that the musicians were all of a uniform darkness of hue, and that they, genuine negroes as they were, had 'blackened up,' the more closely to resemble the professional negro minstrel."

The dignified and imposing Mr. Johnston has sat during all these years in the centre of a long line of black comedians, which includes such artists as "Eph" Horn, "Dan" Neil, and "Jerry" Bryant--whose real name was O'Brien--Charles H. Fox, "Charley" White, George Christy, "Nelse" Seymour--Thomas Nelson Sanderson--the Buckleys, J. W. Raynor, Birch, Bernard, Wambold, Backus, "Pony" Moore, "Dan" Cotton, "Bob" Hart, "Cool" White, "Dan" Emmett, "Dave" Reed, "Matt" Peel, "Ben" Gardner, Luke Schoolcraft, James H. Budworth, Kelly, Leon, "Frank" Brower, S. C. Campbell, "Gus" Howard, "Billy" Newcomb, "Billy" Gray, Aynsley Cooke, "Hughey" Dougherty, "Tony" Hart, Unsworth, W. H. Delehanty, "Sam" Devere, "Add" Ryman, George Thatcher, "Master Eugene," "Ricardo," "Andy" Leavitt, "Sam" Sanford, "Lew" Benedict, "Harry" Bloodgood, "Cal" Wagner, "Ben" Collins, and "Little Mac."

Nothing like a personal history of any of these men, who have been so prominent upon the negro minstrel stage during the half-century of its existence, can be given here. They have all done much to make the world happier and brighter for a time by their public careers, and they have left a pleasant and a cheerful memory behind them. Their gibes, their gambols, their songs, their flashes of merriment, still linger in our eyes and in our ears; and before many readers scores of quaint figures with blackened faces will no doubt dance to half-forgotten tunes all over these pages, which are too crowded to contain more than the mere mention of their names.

How much of the wonderful success and popularity of the negro minstrel is due to the minstrel, how much to the negro melody he introduced, and how much to the characteristic bones, banjo, and tambourine upon which he accompanied himself, is an open question. It was certainly the song, not the singer, which moved Thackeray to write years ago: "I heard a humorous balladist not long since, a minstrel with wool on his head, and an ultra Ethiopian complexion, who performed a negro ballad that I confess moistened these spectacles in a most unexpected manner. I have gazed at thousands of tragedy queens dying on the stage and expiring in appropriate blank-verse, and I never wanted to wipe them. They have looked up, be it said, at many scores of clergymen without being dimmed, and behold! a vagabond with a corked face and a banjo sings a little song, strikes a wild note, which sets the heart thrilling with happy pity."

This ballad perhaps was "Nelly Bly," or "Nelly was
a Lady," or "Lucy Long," or "Oh, Susanna," or
"Nancy Till," or, better than any of these, Stephen
Foster's "Way Down upon the Swanee River," a
song that has touched more hearts than "Annie
Laurie" itself; for, after all, "The Girl We Left
Behind Us" is not more precious in our eyes than
"The Old Folks at Home;" and the American has
sunk very low indeed of whom it cannot be said that
"he never shook his mother." Foster is utterly
unappreciated by his fellow-countrymen, who erect
all their monuments to the men who make their
laws. He was the author of "Massa's in the Cold,
Cold Ground," "Old Dog Tray," "Old Uncle Ned,"
"Old Folks at Home," "Old Kentucky Home,"
"Willie, We have Missed You," and "Come where
My Love lies Dreaming." He died as he had lived,
in 1864, when he was but thirty-seven years of age,
and his "Hard Times Will Come Again No More."

Joel Chandler Harris, who is one of the best friends
the plantation negro ever had, and who certainly
knows him thoroughly, startled the whole
community by writing to the *Critic*, in the autumn
of 1883, that he had never seen a banjo or a
tambourine or a pair of bones in the hands of the
negroes on any of the plantations of middle Georgia
with which he is familiar; that they made sweet
music with the quills, as Pan did; that they played
passably well on the fiddle, the fife, the flute, and
the bugle; that they beat enthusiastically on the
triangle; but that they knew not at all the
instruments tradition had given them. That Uncle
Remus, cannot "pick" the banjo, and never even
heard it "picked," seems hardly credible; but Mr.

Harris knows. Uncle Remus, however, is not a
travelled darky, and the existence of the banjo in
other parts of the South has been clearly proved.
Mr. Cable quotes a creole negro ditty of before the
war in which "Musieu Bainjo" is mentioned on
every line. Maurice Thompson says the banjo is a
common instrument among the field hands in North
Georgia, Alabama, and Tennessee; and he describes
a rude banjo manufactured by its dusky performer
out of a flat gourd, strung with horse-hair; while we
find in Thomas Jefferson's *Notes on Virginia*,
printed in 1784, the following statement: "In music
they [the blacks] are more generally gifted than the
whites with accurate ears for tune and time, and
they have been found capable of imagining a small
catch." In a foot-note Jefferson adds, "The
instrument proper to them is the banjar, which they
brought hither from Africa."

The negro minstrel will give up his tambourine, for
it is as old as the days of the Exodus, when Miriam
the prophetess, the sister of Aaron, took a timbrel in
her hand, and all the women went out after her with
timbrels and with dances; and he will give up the
bones, for Miss Olive Logan, in *Harper's Magazine*
for April, 1879, traces them back to the reign of Fou
Hi, Emperor of China, 3468 B.C., while Shakspere's
King of the Fairies, who made an ass of the hard-
handed man of Athens, also treated Bottom to the
melody of the bones. He will hang up his fiddle and
his bow when the time comes, cheerfully enough,
for Nero, according to tradition, fiddled for the
dancing of the flames that consumed Rome nineteen
hundred years ago. None of these are exclusively
his own; but it would be very cruel to take from him

his banjo, which he evolved if he did not invent,
and without which he can be and can do nothing.

ACT III.

THE AMERICAN BURLESQUE.

THE AMERICAN BURLESQUE.

"The best in this kind are but shadows, and the worst are no worse, if imagination amend them." *A Midsummer-Night's Dream*, Act v. Sc. 1.

The burlesque among serious writers has a bad reputation. George Eliot, in *Theophrastus Such*, says that it debases the moral currency; and George Crabb, in his *English Synonymes*, thus dismisses it: "Satire and irony are the most ill-natured kinds of wit; burlesque stands in the lowest rank."

Burlesque, from the Italian *burlare*, "to joke," "to banter," "to play," has been defined as "an expression of language, a display of gesture, an impression of countenance, the intention being to excite laughter." In art caricature is burlesque, in literature parody is burlesque, in the drama comic pantomime, comic opera, travesty, and extravaganza are burlesque. All dramatic burlesque ranges under the head of farce, although all farce is not burlesque. Burlesque is the farce of portraiture on the stage; farce on the stage is the burlesque of events. Bret Harte's *Condensed Novels* and George Arnold's *McArone Papers* are representative specimens of burlesque in American letters; Arthur B. Frost's famous domestic cat, who supped inadvertently upon rat poison, is an excellent example of burlesque in American art. What America has done for burlesque on the stage it is the aim of the following pages to show.

Hipponax, of Ephesus, who lived in the latter half of the sixth century before Christ, is credited with having been "The Father of Burlesque Poetry." He was small and ill-favored physically, and his natural personal defects were the indirect cause of the development of his satirical powers and of his posthumous fame. Two sculptors of Chios caricatured him grossly in a statue publicly exhibited, and he, in return, fired his muse with the torch of hatred, and burned them in effigy with terrible but clever ridicule. He parodied the *Iliad*, in which he made Achilles an Ionian glutton; he did not spare his own parents; he poked fun at the gods themselves; he impaled Mrs. Hipponax with a couplet upon which she is still exhibited to the scoffers, and he is only to be distinguished from his long line of successors by the curious fact that he does not seem to have spoken with derision of his mother-in-law! His tribute to matrimony is still preserved in choice iambics, roughly translated as follows: "There are but two happy days in the life of a married man--the day of his marriage, and the day of the burial of his wife." From this it will be seen that twenty-five centuries or more look down upon the Benedict of the modern burlesque, who leaves his wife at home when he travels for pleasure!

Aristophanes, the comic poet of Athens, who wrote fifty-four comedies between the years 427 and 388 B.C., may be termed "The Father of the Burlesque Play." He satirized people more than things, or than

other men's tragedies, and to his school belong
Brougham's *Pocahontas* and *Columbus*, rather than
the same author's *Dan Keyser de Bassoon*, or *Much
Ado About a Merchant of Venice*. The plots of
Aristophanes are as original as his wit. In *The
Wasps* he caricatured the fondness of the Athenians
for litigation; in *The Birds* his object was to
convince the Athenians of the advantages of a clean
political sweep; in *The Female Orators* he satirized
the Sorosis and the women suffragists of his time;
in *The Feast of Ceres* he pointed out how useful and
ornamental woman is in her own sphere; and in
Peace, written to urge the close of the
Peloponnesian war, he reached the sublimity of
burlesque in creating a stage heroine who never
utters a word. The argument of *The Knights* will
give a very fair idea of the plots of his plays. Athens
is represented as a private house, whose master,
Demos (the people), has more servants and more
servants' relations than he can comfortably wait
upon or decently support. Nicias and Demosthenes
are his slaves, and Cleon, a political boss of the
period, is his butler and confidential valet. Demos is
irritable, superstitious, inconstant in his pursuits,
and dull in character. Agoracritus, a sausage-seller,
subverts the plots and the plans of the demagogue
Cleon--originally played by Aristophanes himself--
shows the householder that his favorite servant is
utterly unworthy of the public trust, and brings the
entertainment to a close with the discomfiture of the
Ring and the relief of the taxpayers. Demos is said
to have been the prototype of "John Bull," the
personification of the Englishman, as he was first
exhibited by Dr. Arbuthnot in the early part of the
eighteenth century, and *The Knights* is regarded as

"an historical piece of great value, because it furnishes a faithful picture of the nation and of its customs." What curious ideas of American life and manners will posterity gather from *Adonis* and *Evangeline*!

Classical critics credit Aristophanes with being distinguished for the exuberance of his wit, for his inexhaustible fund of comic humor, and for the Attic purity and great simplicity of his language; while at the same time he is accused of introducing, when it suits his purpose, every variety of dialect, of coining new words and expressions as occasion offers, and of making bad puns, whether occasion offers or not; in all of which his disciples persistently and consistently follow him.

Samuel Foote, who lived in an age of epithets, was called "The British Aristophanes." He respected no person and no thing. He satirized every subject, sacred or profane, which struck his fancy, from Chesterfield's Letters to the Stratford Jubilee; and he caricatured everybody, from Whitfield to the Duchess of Kingston. His serious attempt at Othello, in the beginning of his career as an actor, was considered a master-piece of unconscious burlesque, only inferior, in its extravagance and nonsense, to his Hamlet, and he failed in every legitimate part he undertook to play. As a mimic, however, in dramatic productions of his own writing, he met with immense success; and as a writer of stage burlesque he ranks very high. He made Italian opera ridiculous in his *Cat Concert*; he gave serious offence to a hard-working, respectable trade in *The Tailors, a Tragedy for Warm Weather*;

he attacked the medical profession in *The Devil on Two Sticks*; he parodied sentimental romance of the *Pamela* school in his *Piety in Pattens*; and he offended all right-thinking persons, heterodox as well as orthodox, in *The Minor*, a travesty upon the methods of Wesley and his Church.

The Most Lamentable Comedy and Most Cruell Death of Pyramus and Thisbie, originally published in the year 1600, if not the earliest burlesque in the English language, is certainly the model upon which are based all subsequent productions of the same class which have been written for the British or American theatre. Stevens believes the title to have been suggested to Shakspere by Dr. Thomas Preston's *Lamentable Tragedy Mixed Ful of Pleasant Mirth--Conteyning the Life of Cambises, King of Percia*. The story of Pyramus and Thisbe is to be found in the fourth book of Ovid's *Metamorphoses*; and a volume called *Perymus and Thesbye* was entered on the Stationers' Register in 1562-63. Arthur Golding's translation of Ovid was published in 1567, and several other versions of the tale were extant before the birth of Snout or Bottom, the incidents, of course, being the same in all. Shaksperean scholars find traces of other works in the different speeches of the hard-handed men of Athens, but the general impression is that the author's purpose was to travesty the verse of Golding. Limander and Helen are intended for Leander and Hero; Shafalus and Procrus for Cephalus and Procris, and Ninny for Ninus; a form of verbal contortion displayed by the modern burlesquer in *Sam Parr* for *Zampa*, and *The Roof Scrambler* for *Sonnambula*; while the lines--

"Whereat, with blade, with bloody, blamefull blade,
He brauely broacht his boiling bloody breast,"

read like the blank-verse mouthed by the deep
tragedians of the negro minstrel stage of to-day.

The Midsummer-Night's Dream, with Mr. Hilson as
Snout and Mr. Placide as Bottom, was performed,
"for the first time in America," at the Park Theatre,
New York, on the 9th of November, 1826, when the
stage in this country was upwards of three-quarters
of a century old, and had a literature of its own,
comparatively rich in comedy and tragedy, and
when its burlesque, such as it was, undoubtedly felt
the influence of *Pyramus and Thisbe*.

The second great burlesque upon the British stage
was *The Rehearsal*, by George Villiers, Duke of
Buckingham, in the reign of the Second Charles,
first acted in 1672. It was original in design and
brilliant in execution. It introduced a popular
author, John Dryden, engaged in superintendence of
a rehearsal of one of his own tragedies--the tragedy
in this instance consisting of clever parodies of
portions of all the dramas then in vogue. *The
Rehearsal* does not seem to have been produced in
this country, although *The Critic* of Sheridan,
obviously based upon it, was performed at the John
Street Theatre, New York, November 24th, 1788,
when President Washington honored the
entertainment with his presence. The cast has not
been preserved, although William Winter believes
Mr. Wignell to have played Puff, Mr. Ryan
Whiskerandos, and Mrs. Morris (the second wife of
Owen Morris) Tilberina. *The Critic* still survives, as

Mr. Daly's audiences well remember.

Burlesque upon the American stage, although not
yet American burlesque, dates back to the very
beginning of the history of the theatre in this
country, when *The Beggar's Opera*, by John Gay,
"written in ridicule of the musical Italian drama,"
was presented at the theatre in Nassau Street, New
York, on the 3d of December, 1750, with Thomas
Kean as Captain Macheath. *The Beggar's Opera*
was first acted at Lincoln's Inn Fields in 1727, and
took the town by storm. The Archbishop of
Canterbury preached a sermon against it; Sir John
Fielding, the police-justice, officially begged the
manager not to present it on *Saturday evenings*, as it
inspired the idle apprentices of London, who saw it
on their night off, to imitate its hero's thieving
deeds; and a certain critic condemned it as "the
parent of that most monstrous of all absurdities, the
comic opera." Nevertheless it was immensely
popular, and enjoyed an unusually long run. As a
literary production it is distinguished for its
combination of nature, pathos, satire, and burlesque.
It brought fame to its author, and, indirectly,
something like wealth; and it made a duchess of
Lavinia Fenton, who was the original Polly. As that
monstrous absurdity the comic opera is without
question the parent of that still more monstrous
absurdity the burlesque proper, Polly Peachum and
Captain Macheath may be considered the very
Pilgrim Parents of burlesque in the New World.
They were followed almost immediately (February
25, 1751) by *Damon and Phillada, a Ballad Farce*,
by Colley Cibber. Their Plymouth Rock very soon
became too small to hold them; their descendants

have taken possession of the whole land, and every *Mayflower* that crosses the Atlantic to-day brings consignments of British blondes to swell their number. Before the Revolution Fielding's *Tom Thumb; or, The Tragedy of Tragedies*, a clever travesty, with Mrs. Hallam (Mrs. Douglas) as Queen Dollalolla, and Kane O'Hara's *Midas*, "a burlesque turning upon heathen deities, ridiculous enough in themselves, and too absurd for burlesque," had taken out their naturalization papers. *The Critic*, as has been shown, declared his intentions very shortly after the establishment of peace; and *Bombastes Furioso* became a citizen of New York as early as 1816.

As Satan in the proverb builds invariably a chapel hard by the house of prayer, so does the demon of burlesque as surely erect his hovel next door to the palace of the legitimate tragedian. He spoils by his absurd architecture every neighborhood he enters; he even cuts off the views from the Castle of Elsinore, and disfigures the approaches to the royal tombs of the ancient Danish kings. John Poole's celebrated travesty of *Hamlet*, one of the earliest of its kind, was first published in London in 1811. George Holland, afterwards so popular upon the American stage for many years, presented Poole's play on the occasion of his first benefit in this country, March 22, 1828, appearing himself as the First Grave-digger and as Ophelia. This was about the beginning of what, for want of a better term, may be styled "legitimate burlesque" in the United States. It inspired our managers to import, and our native authors to write, travesties upon everything in the standard drama which was serious and ought

to have been respected; and it led to burlesques of
*Antony and Cleopatra, Douglas, Macbeth, Othello,
Romeo and Juliet, Manfred, The Tempest, Valentine
and Orson, Richard the Third, The Hunchback*, and
many more; and between the years 1839, when
William Mitchell opened the Olympic, and 1859,
when William E. Burton made his last bow to the
New York public, was laid out and built between
Chambers Street and the site of Brougham's
Lyceum, on Broadway, corner of Broome Street,
that metropolis of burlesque upon the ruins of
which the dramatic antiquary, whose name is Palmy
Days, now loves to sit and ponder.

The titles of its half-forgotten streets and buildings,
collected at random from its old directories, then
known as the bills of the play, will recall pleasant
memories and excite gentle wonder. There were,
among others, *A Lad in a Wonderful Lamp, The
Bohea Man's Girl, Fried Shots* [*Freischütz*]*, Her
Nanny, Lucy Did Sham Her Moor*, and *Lucy Did
Lamm Her Moor, Man Fred, Cinder Nelly, Wench
Spy, Spook Wood, Buy It Dear, 'Tis Made of
Cashmere* [*Bayadere; or, The Maid of Cashmere*]*,
The Cat's in the Larder, or, The Maid with the
Parasol* [*La Gazza Ladra; or, The Maiden of
Paillaisseau*]*, The Humpback, Mrs. Normer*, and
Richard Number Three.

Of this metropolis William Mitchell was the first
Lord Mayor. He was the inaugurator, if not the
creator, of an entirely new school of dramatic
architecture, which was as general, and sometimes
as absurd, as the style which has since spread over
the country at the expense of the reputation of good

Queen Anne; and he led the popular taste for a
number of years, to the great enjoyment of his
clients, if not to their mental profit. William
Horncastle, a good singer and a fair actor, and Dr.
William K. Northall were his assistants in dramatic
construction, and the authors of many of his
extravagant productions. One of his earliest and
most popular burlesques was entitled *La Mosquito*.
It was based upon *The Tarantula* of Fanny Elssler,
and was presented at the close of his first season.
An extract from the bill will give a fair idea of the
quality of the fooling:

"First time in this or any other country, a new comic
burlesque ballet, entitled *La Mosquito*, in which
Monsieur Mitchell will make his first appearance as
une Première Danseuse, and show his agility in a
variety of terpsichorean efforts of all sorts in the
genuine Bolerocachucacacavonienne style.... The
ballet is founded on the well-known properties of
the mosquito, whose bites render the patient
exceedingly impatient, and throws him into a fit of
slapping and scratching and swearing delirium,
commonly termed the '*Cacoethes Scratchendi*,'
causing the unfortunate being to cut capers enough
for a considerable number of legs of mutton. The
scene lies in Hoboken," etc.

Concerning Mitchell's performance, Dr. Northall
writes, in *Before and Behind the Curtain*: "We shall
long remember the comic humor with which he
burlesqued the charming and graceful Fanny. The
manner of his exit from the stage at the conclusion
of the dance was irresistibly comic, and the serious
care with which he guided himself to the side

scenes, to secure a passage for his tremendous bustle, was very funny."

Mr. Mitchell's other famous burlesque parts were Man Fred, Hamlet, Willy Walters (in *The Humpback*), Sam Parr, Jap (in *Loves of the Angels*), Antony, and Richard Number Three. Very few portraits of this old actor, either in character or otherwise, are known to the collectors. The accompanying print is from a drawing made by Charles Parsons while seated in the pit of the old Olympic half a century ago, when the draughtsman--a mere lad--was beginning his professional career. The original sketch was given to Mr. Mitchell by the young artist, who received in return a pass to the theatre--the highest ambition of the boys of that period.

Mitchell was forced to retire from the mayoralty before the close of his last season at the Olympic, in 1849-50, having been deposed the previous year by William E. Burton at the Chambers Street house. As Lester Wallack said in his *Memories*, Burton did everything that Mitchell did, and did it in a better way, with better players and better plays. His first burlesque was a cruel treatment of the opera of *Lucia*, followed immediately by a heartless travesty of Dibdin's *Valentine and Orson*. These were succeeded by *The Tempest*, in which Mrs. Brougham (Miss Nelson), a lady of enormous physical size, played Ariel. A little while later Mr. Brougham played Macbeth to the Macduff of Thomas B. Johnstone, the Banquo of Oliver B. Raymond, and the Lady Macbeth of Burton himself. Mark Smith made a fascinating Norma, Leffingwell played the Stern Parient in *Villikens and his Dinah*, and Charles Fisher, in white tights, a tunic, gauze wings, and a flowing wig, pirouetted with Mrs. Skerrett in a production called *St. Cupid*, in which Mr. Burton appeared as Queen Bee, a Gypsy Woman.

It would be an easy matter to fill many of these pages with stories of the humorous productions and the laughable performances of Burton and Brougham on the Chambers Street boards. The literature of the American theatre overflows with anecdotes of their quarrels and their reconciliations upon the stage, their jokes upon each other, their impromptu wit, their unexpected "gags"--which were always looked for--the liberties they took with their authors, their audiences, and themselves, and, above all, with their incomparable acting in every part, whether it was serious or frivolous.

The last, and in many respects the greatest, of the trio of actors, authors, and managers who may be considered the founders of American burlesque, began his brilliant but brief reign at the Lyceum, at Broome Street, late in 1850, about the time of the retirement of Mitchell, and long before his later rival, Burton, was ready to lay down his sceptre. If America has ever had an Aristophanes, John Brougham was his name. His *Pocahontas* and *Columbus* are almost classics. They rank among the best, if they are not the very best, burlesques in any living language. Their wit is never coarse, they ridicule nothing which is not a fit subject for ridicule, they outrage no serious sentiment, they hurt no feelings, they offend no portion of the community, they shock no modesty, they never blaspheme; and, as Dr. Benjamin Ellis Martin has happily expressed it, their author was "the first to give to burlesque its crowning comic conceit of utter earnestness, of solemn seriousness."

The Lyceum was opened on the 23d of December, 1850, with "an occasional rigmarole entitled *Brougham, and Co.*," which introduced the entire company to the public. The next absurdity was *A Row at the Lyceum*, with Mr. Florence in the gallery, Mr. Brougham himself in the pit, and the rest of the *dramatis personæ* upon the stage; and shortly before the abrupt close of Mr. Brougham's management he presented *What Shall We Do for Something New?* in which Mrs. Brougham appeared as Rudolpho, Mrs. Skerrett as Elvino, and Mr. Johnstone as Amina, in a travesty upon *La Sonnambula.*

Upon the same stage, on Christmas Eve, 1855, but under the management of the elder Wallack, Brougham produced his "Original, Aboriginal, Erratic, Operatic, Semi-civilized, and Demi-savage Extravaganza of *Pocahontas.*" The scenery, as announced, was painted from daguerreotypes and other authentic documents, the costumes were cut from original plates, and the music was dislocated and reset, by the heads of the different departments of the theatre. Charles Walcot played John Smith, "according to this story, but somewhat in variance with his story"; Miss Hodson played the titular part, and Mr. Brougham represented "Pow-Ha-Tan I., King of the Tuscaroras--a Crotchety Monarch, in fact a Semi-Brave." At the close of the opening song (to the air of "Hoky-poky-winky-wum") he thus addressed his people:

"Well roared, indeed, my jolly Tuscaroras. Most loyal corps, your King encores your chorus;"

and until the fall of the curtain, at the end of the second and last act, the scintillations of wit and the thunder of puns were incessant and startling. "May I ask," says Col-o-gog (J. H. Stoddart), "in the word *lie*, what vowel do you use, sir, *i* or *y*?"

"Y, sir, or I, sir, search the vowels through, And find the one most consonant to you."

Later the King cries:

"Sergeant-at-arms, say, what alarms the crowd; Loud noise annoys us; why is it allowed?"

And Captain Smith, describing his first introduction at the royal court, says:

"I visited his Majesty's abode, A portly savage, plump and pigeon-toed; Like Metamora, both in feet and feature, I never met-a-more-a-musing creature."

In a more serious but not less happy vein is the apostrophe to tobacco, by the smoking, joking Powhatan, as follows:

"While other joys one sense alone can measure, This to all senses gives ecstatic pleasure. You *feel*

the radiance of the glowing bowl, *Hear* the soft
murmurs of the kindling coal, *Smell* the sweet
fragrance of the honey-dew, *Taste* its strong
pungency the palate through, *See* the blue cloudlets
circling to the dome, Imprisoned skies up-floating
to their home-- I like a dhudeen myself!"

And so he joked and smoked his way into a
popularity which no stage monarch has enjoyed
before or since. *Pocahontas* ran for many weeks,
and was frequently repeated for many years. The
story of the sudden departure of the original
Pocahontas one night without a word of warning,
and the successful performance of the piece by
Brougham and Walcot, with no one to play the
titular part at all, is as familiar in the theatrical
annals as the sadder stories of Woffington's last
appearance, and the death of Palmer on the stage;
and no doubt it will be remembered long after
Pocahontas itself, despite its cleverness, is quite
forgotten.

"*Columbus el Filibustero*, a New and Audaciously
Original, Historico-plagiaristic, Ante-national, Pre-
patriotic, and Omni-local Confusion of
Circumstances. Running through Two Acts and
Four Centuries," was first performed at Burton's
Theatre (Broadway, opposite Bond Street,
afterwards the Winter Garden) on the 31st of
December, 1857; Mark Smith playing Ferdinand,
Lawrence Barrett Talavera, Miss Lizzie Weston
Davenport Columbia, and Mr. Brougham himself
Columbus. It is a more serious production than
Pocahontas; the satire is more subtle, and the
thought more delicate. It contains no play upon

words, is not filled with startling absurdities, and is pathetic rather than uproariously funny. While *Pocahontas* inspires nothing but laughter, *Columbus* excites sympathy, and oftentimes he has moved his audiences to the verge of tears. He is a much-abused, simple, honest old man, full of sublime ideas, and long ahead of his times. He dreams prophetic dreams, and in his visions he

"sees a land Where Nature seems to frame with practised hand Her last most wondrous work. Before him rise Mountains of solid rock that rift the skies, Imperial valleys with rich verdure crowned For leagues illimitable smile around, While through them subject seas for rivers run From ice-bound tracks to where the tropic sun Breeds in the teeming ooze strange monstrous things. He sees, upswelling from exhaustless springs, Great lakes appear, upon whose surface wide The banded navies of the earth may ride. He sees tremendous cataracts emerge From cloud-aspiring heights, whose slippery verge Tremendous oceans momently roll o'er, Assaulting with unmitigated roar The stunned and shattered ear of trembling day, That, wounded, weeps in glistening tears of spray."

In short, he sees so much that is beyond the comprehension of the ordinary play-goer, that for thirty years he has been left in absolute retirement in that Forrest Home for good old plays which is styled *French's Minor Drama.*

One of Brougham's last burlesque productions was his *Much Ado About a Merchant of Venice,* presented March 8, 1869, at the little theatre on

Twenty-fourth Street, New York, which has since
borne so many names, and now, rebuilt, is known as
the Madison Square. He played Shylock, Miss Effie
Germon Lorenzo, and Mrs. J. J. Prior Portia. This
was his final effort at theatrical management. He
appeared in *Pocahontas* as late as 1876, but
Shylock was his last original burlesque part which
is worthy of serious mention.

Francis Talfourd's *Shylock; or, The Merchant of
Venice Preserved, a Jerusalem Hearty Joke*, is a
much older production than Brougham's travesty of
the same play, with which it should not be
confounded. Frederic Robson was the original
Shylock in London, Tom Johnstone in New York
(at Burton's, October 9, 1853). M. W. Leffingwell
gave an admirable performance of Talfourd's
Shylock in September, 1867, on the stage of this
same little Twenty-fourth Street theatre, assisted by
Miss Lina Edwin as Jessica. Mr. Leffingwell was a
very versatile actor although he excelled in
burlesque and broadly extravagant parts. He will be
remembered as Romeo Jaffier Jenkins, in *Too Much
for Good Nature*, and in travesties of *Cinderella*
and *Fra Diavolo*. In the last absurdity, as Beppo,
made up in very clever imitation of Forrest as the
Gladiator, and enormously padded, he strutted
about the stage for many moments, entirely
unconscious of a large carving-fork stuck into the
sawdust which formed the calf of his gladiatorial
leg. His look of agony and his roar of anguish--
perfect reflections of Forrest's voice and action--
when his attention was called to his physical
suffering, made one of the most ludicrous scenes in
the whole history of American burlesque. Mr.

Forrest is said to have remarked of a lithograph of Leffingwell in this part, that while the portrait of himself was not so bad, the characteristics were somewhat exaggerated! Leffingwell was, no doubt, the original of the full length, life-sized effigy of Forrest which serves as the sign for a cigar store on one of the leading thoroughfares of New York to-day.

Madame Tostée, in 1867, with the *Grand Duchess*, and Miss Lydia Thompson, the next season, with *Ixion*--although neither of these can be considered American burlesques--gave new life to burlesque in America; and for a number of years burlesque was rampant upon the American stage; many leading comedians of later days, who will hardly be associated with that style of performance by the theatre-goers of the present generation, devoting themselves to travestie and extravaganza. Among the most successful of these may be mentioned William J. Florence, Stuart Robson, James Lewis, and Harry Beckett. The last gentleman was exceedingly comic, and at the same time always refined and artistic in such parts as Minerva in *Ixion*, Hassarac in *The Forty Thieves*, the Widow Twankey in *Aladdin*, Maid Marian in *Robin Hood*, and Queen Elizabeth in *Kenilworth* long before he became the established low comedian of Mr. Lester Wallack's company, and won such well-merited popularity by his clever representations of characters as divergent as Tony Lumpkin, Harvey Duff, in *The Shaughraun*, and Mark Meddle.

In January, 1869, Mr. and Mrs. Florence played an engagement of extravaganza at Wood's Museum--

now Daly's Theatre--on Broadway, near Thirtieth Street, presenting *The Field of the Cloth of Gold*, in which Mr. Florence assumed the character of Francis First, Louis Mestayer Henry Eighth, Mrs. Florence Lady Constance, Miss Lillie Eldridge La Sieur de Boissy, and Miss Rose Massey (her first appearance in America) Lord Darnley. The feature of this performance, naturally, was the grand tournament upon the plain between Ardres and Guisnes, in which the rival monarchs fought for the international championship with boxing gloves in the roped arena, and according to the rules of the prize-ring, the police finally breaking up the match and carrying both combatants into the ignominious lockup. Older play-goers will remember Mr. Florence years before this as Eily O'Conner, in a burlesque of *The Colleen Bawn*, and as Beppo "a very Heavy Villain of the Bowery Drama in Kirby's days," in *Fra Diavolo*, Mrs. Florence making a marvellous Danny Mann in the former piece.

While Mr. Florence was taking gross liberties with the personality of Francis First at Wood's, Mr. Lewis was doing cruel injustice to the character of Lucretia Borgia at the Waverley Theatre, 720 Broadway, under the management of Miss Elise Holt, who played Gennaro. The palace of the Borgias was "set" as a modern apothecary's shop, where poison was sold in large or small quantities, and Mr. Lewis excited roars of laughter as a quack doctress, with great capabilities of advertising herself and her nostrums. During the same engagement Mr. Lewis played Rebecca in *Ivanhoe*, and Oenone in *Paris*; but he joined Mr. Daly's company a few months later, and the legitimate has since marked him for its own.

At the Fifth Avenue Theatre, and afterwards at Wallack's, in this same summer of 1869, Stuart Robson made a great hit as Captain Crosstree, in F. C. Burnand's travesty of *Black-eyed Susan*, a part originally played in this country during the previous season by Mark Smith. Mr. Robson had the support of Harry Pearson as Doggrass, of Miss Kitty Blanchard as William, and of Miss Mary Cary as Susan. The entertainment, as a whole, was unusually good, full of exquisite drollery and grotesque fancy, although Captain Crosstree eclipsed every other feature. His "make up" was a marvel of absurdity, his naturally slight figure was literally blown to an enormous size, the contrast between his immense physical rotundity and his thin, inimitably squeaky little voice being exceedingly ludicrous.

During this season the Lydia Thompson troupe was in the full tide of its success; William Horace Lingard and Miss Alice Dunning were playing *Pluto* and *Orpheus in New York*; every negro minstrel and variety performer was burlesquing some person or some thing every night in the week, and opera-bouffe had taken possession of half of the theatres in the land.

The most successful burlesque of those times, and the entertainment which is most fresh in the memory, was "The New Version of Shakspere's Masterpiece of *Hamlet*, as arranged by T. C. De Leon, of Mobile, for George L. Fox," and first presented in New York at the Olympic (formerly

Laura Keene's) Theatre, on Broadway, February 14, 1870. Although not an improvement upon the original acting version of the tragedy, it was an improvement upon the general run of burlesques of its generation; it did not depend upon lime-lights or upon anatomical display, and it did not harrow up the young blood of its auditors by its horrible plays upon unoffending words. It followed the text of Shakspere closely enough to preserve the plot of the story; it contained, as well, a great deal that was ludicrous and bright, and it never sank into imbecility or indelicacy, which is saying much for a burlesque. Mr. Fox, one of the few really funny men of his day upon the American stage, was at his best in this travesty of *Hamlet*. Quite out of the line of the pantomimic clown by which he is now remembered, it was as supremely absurd, as expressed upon his face and in his action, as was his *Humpty Dumpty*. It was perhaps more a burlesque of Edwin Booth--after whom in the character he played and dressed--than of Hamlet, and probably no one enjoyed this more thoroughly, or laughed at it more heartily, than did Mr. Booth himself. While Fox at times was wonderfully like Booth in attitude, look, and voice, he would suddenly assume the accent and expression of Fechter, whom he counterfeited admirably, and again give a most intense passage in the wonderfully deep tones of Studley, at the Bowery. To see Mr. Fox pacing the platform before the Castle of Elsinore, protected against the eager and the nipping air of the night by a fur cap and collar, and with mittens and arctic overshoes, over the traditional costume of Hamlet; to see the woful melancholy of his face as he spoke the most absurd of lines; to watch the horror expressed upon his countenance when the Ghost appeared; to hear his familiar conversation with that Ghost, and his untraditional profanity when commanded by the Ghost to "swear"--all expressed, now in the style of Fechter, now of Studley, now of Booth--was as thoroughly and ridiculously enjoyable as any piece of acting our stage has seen since Burton and Mitchell were at their funniest, so many years before. He was startling in his recommendation of a brewery as a place of refuge for Ophelia, and in the church-yard his "business" was new and quite original, particularly the apostrophe to the skull of Yorick, who, he seemed to think, was laughing now on the wrong side of his face. Fox was one of the earliest Hamlets to realize that the skull even of a jester, when it has lain in the earth three-and-twenty years, is not a pleasant object to touch or smell, although very interesting in itself to point a moral, or for its association's sake; and the expression of his face, as he threw the skull of the dead jester at the quick head of the First Grave-digger, was more suggestive to the close observer of the base uses to which we may all return than any "Alas, poor Yorick!" ever uttered.

Hamlet at the Olympic was played for ten consecutive weeks. The general cast was not particularly strong or remarkable, except in the Ophelia of Miss Belle Howett. She was serious, and surprisingly effective in the mad scene, and often the superior of many of the representatives of Ophelia in the original tragedy, who unwittingly have burlesqued what the burlesque actress, perhaps as unwittingly, played conscientiously and well.

The travesty of *Hamlet* by Mr. Fox is dwelt upon
particularly here as being in many respects one of
the best the American stage has ever seen, and as
giving the present writer an opportunity of paying
just tribute to the memory of an actor who, like so
many of his professional brethren, was never
properly appreciated during his life, and who never
before--not even in William Winter's usually
complete *Brief Chronicles*--has received more than
a passing notice in the long records of the stage he
did so much to adorn.

George L. Fox was not always the clown and
pantomimist of the *Humpty Dumpty* absurdity in
which he is now remembered. He excelled in
burlesque, as his Hamlet and Richelieu and
Macbeth have shown. As a Shaksperean comedian
his Bottom ranks among the best within the memory
of men still living, while in standard low comedy,
melodramatic, and even in tragedy parts, he had no
little experience and some decided success. He
made his first appearance in 1830 at the Tremont
Street Theatre, in Boston, when he was but five
years of age. The play was *The Children of the Alps*,
and the occasion a benefit to Charles Kean. He
played Phineas Fletcher, in the drama of *Uncle
Tom's Cabin*, during its famous run of so many
nights at the National Theatre, New York, in 1853-
54. He excelled as Mark Meddle, as Trip, as
Jacques Strop, in *Robert Macaire*, as Tom Tape, in
Sketches in India, as Box, as Cox, and as Sundown
Bowse, in *Horizon*.

Bottom was his most finished and artistic
assumption, Hamlet probably his most amusing, and

Humpty Dumpty his most successful. He played the
latter part some fifteen hundred times in New York
and elsewhere. It was the last part he ever attempted
to play, and only as a clown does he exist in the
minds of the men of to-day who think of him at all.
He first appeared in New York at the National
Theatre, in 1850; he was last seen at Booth's
Theatre on the 25th of November, 1875--the saddest
clown who ever chalked his face. After twenty
years of constant, faithful service as public jester--
shattered in health, broken in spirit, shaken in mind-
-he disappeared forever from public view. Alas,
poor Yorick!

One of the most popular as well as the longest lived
of the contemporary burlesques is *Evangeline*, in
the construction or reconstruction of which Mr.
Brougham is known to have had a share. As a
travesty upon a purely American subject, originally
treated, of course, in all seriousness by an illustrious
American, Mr. Longfellow, and at the suggestion of
an American equally illustrious, Mr. Hawthorne,
Evangeline may surely claim to be an aboriginal
production; it merits its success, and with a certain
degree of national pride it may be recorded here that
it has been repeated upon the American stage over
five thousand times. In it, at the Fifth Avenue
Theatre, in Twenty-eighth Street, New York, during
the summer of 1877, Miss Eliza Weathersby, as
Gabrielle, made a pleasant impression, William H.
Crane appeared as Le Blanc, George H. Knight
gave a series of wonderful imitations of the Hero of
New Orleans, N. C. Goodwin came prominently
before the public, and Harry Hunter, although not
the original in the part, created a decided sensation

as the Lone Fisherman, one of the drollest dramatic conceptions of modern times. He had no connection whatever with the play, had not a word to say, was entirely unnoticed by his fellow-players, paid no attention to anybody, but was always present--the first to enter, the last to leave every scene. With his ridiculous costume, his palm-leaf fan, his fishing-rod, his camp-stool, he pervaded everything, was ever prominent, never obtrusive, and exceedingly mirth-provoking. It may be added that Henry Dixey, whose Adonis is one of the best of modern burlesque performances, made, during the long run of *Evangeline*, his New York *début* as the fore-legs of the heifer!

Amusement seekers in the metropolis will remember with pleasure Willie Edouin, Mrs. James Oates, and scores of other burlesque actors, excellent in many ways, whom it will not be possible even to mention here. N. C. Goodwin burlesqued a burlesque at Harrigan and Hart's first theatre, when he played Captain Stuart Robson-Crosstree to the Dame Hadley of Mr. Harrigan and the Black-eyed Susan of Mr. Hart; at the same house G. K. Fortescue played Lousqueeze to Mr. Hart's Hungry-Yet and Mr. Harrigan's Pierre, in a play styled *The Two Awfuls*. The San Francisco Minstrels at the same time presented *The Four Orphans and the Big Banana*, a burlesque upon two dramas of great popularity and no little merit.

The subject of American burlesque can hardly be dismissed here without some brief allusion to a number of very clever parodies seen of late years upon the amateur stage. The poets of the various college associations have turned their muse in the direction of travesty, and with considerable success; one of the best and most popular of the entertainments of the Hasty Pudding Club, the *Dido and Æneas* of Owen Wister, the grandson of Fanny Kemble, being a production worthy of professional talent. John K. Bangs has written for amateur companies *Katherine, The Story of the Shrew*, and *Mephistopheles, a Profanation*. In the first the tamer of Shakspere finds the tables turned, and is himself tamed; while in the latter Faust's mother-in-law, the good fairy of the piece, outwits the evil genius and frustrates his designs; a power of invention on the part of Mr. Bangs which proves him to be, perhaps, the only true son of the Father of Burlesque, Hipponax himself.

But to return to the "palmy days of burlesque," before the period of opera-bouffe, and the coming of the English blondes. When stock companies were the rule, and Mitchell and Burton controlled the stock, singing and dancing were as much a part of every actor's education as elocution and gesture; and it was not considered beneath the dignity of the Rip Van Winkle or the Hamlet of one night to travesty parts equally serious the next. Mr. Booth, early in his career, appeared in such entertainments as *Blue Beard*; and Mr. Jefferson was enormously popular as Beppo, Hiawatha, Pan (in *Midas*), the Tycoon, and Mazeppa--old play-bills recording his appearance as Granby Gag to the Jenny Lind of Mrs. John Wood, "with his original grape-vine twist and burlesque break-down." His performance of Mazeppa at the Winter Garden in 1861 is still a pleasant memory in many minds. In it he sang "his celebrated aria, 'The Victim of Despair'"; and his daring act upon the bare back of the wild rocking-horse of the toy-shops was, perhaps, the most remarkable performance of its kind ever witnessed by a danger-loving public. During his several engagements at the Winter Garden Mr. Jefferson was supported by Mrs. John Wood (particularly as Ivanhoe to his Sir Brian), one of the best burlesque actresses our stage has known. Her Pocahontas was never excelled. She played it at Niblo's to the Powhatan of Mark Smith in March, 1872; and almost her last appearance upon the New York stage was made at the Grand Opera-house in November of the same year, in John Brougham's burlesque *King Carrot*, when that humorist remarked, although not of Mrs. Wood, that he was supported by vegetable "supes."

That burlesque "came natural" to Mr. Jefferson is shown in the wonderful successes of his half-brother, Charles Burke, in burlesque parts. Mr. Burke's admirers, even at the end of thirty-five years, still speak enthusiastically of his comic Iago, of his Clod Meddlenot (in *The Lady of the Lions*), of his Mr. MacGreedy (Mr. Macready), of his Kazrac (in *Aladdin*), and of his Met-a-roarer, in which he gave absurd imitations of Mr. Forrest as the Last of the Wampanoags.

No history of American burlesque could be complete without some mention of the name of Daniel Setchell. His Leah the Forsook, and Mark Smith's Madeline are remembered as pleasantly in New York as his Macbeth and Edwin Adams's Macduff are remembered in Boston. William H.

Crane places the Macduff of Adams--he dressed in the volunteer uniform of the first year of the war, and read lines ridiculous beyond measure with all of the magnificent effect his wonderful voice and perfect elocution could give them--as the finest piece of burlesque acting it has ever been his good-fortune to see. But the stories told by the old comedians of the extravagant comedy performances of their contemporaries in other days, if they could be collected here, would extend this chapter far beyond the limits of becoming space.

Whether the burlesque of the present is comparable with the burlesque of the past is an open question, much debated. Mr. Wilson in the *Oolah*, Mr. Hopper as Juliet, Mr. Powers in *The Marquis*, Mr. Goodwin in *Little Jack Sheppard*, Mr. Burgess as the Widow Bedott--if she can be considered a burlesque part--and other men and women who burlesque women and men and things to-day, are, without question, very clever performers; the laughs they raise are as hearty and prolonged as any which paid tribute to the talents of the comedians who went before them; and it is unjust, perhaps, to judge them by high standards which live only in the memory, and grow higher as distance lends enchantment to their view. As Lawrence Barrett has said, "the actor is a sculptor who carves his image in snow." The burlesque which has melted from our sight seems to us, as we look back at it, to be purer and cleaner than the frozen burlesque upon which the sun as yet has made no impression; and the figure of Pocahontas, gone with the lost arts, seems more beautiful than the Evangeline of the modern school. When the Adonis of the present counterfeits the deep tragedian he is guilty of imitation, and of clever imitation, but nothing more; when he represents the clerk in the country store he gives an admirable piece of comedy acting; but he never rises to the sublime heights of Columbus, as Columbus is remembered by those who saw him before Hoolah Goolah was born.

If American burlesque did not die with John Brougham, it has hardly yet recovered from the shock of his death; and he certainly deserves a colossal statue in its Pantheon.

ACT IV.

INFANT PHENOMENA OF AMERICA.

INFANT PHENOMENA OF AMERICA.

"So cunning, and so young, is wonderful." *Richard III.*, Act iii. Sc. 1.

While the "Grand Spectacle of the *Black Crook*" was enjoying its fourth successful run at Niblo's Garden, New York, in the season of 1873, a precociously bright little musician of some six or seven years of age, so advertised in the bills, and to all appearances no older, preternaturally large in head and small in person, won the affection and the sympathy of all those who witnessed his performances. During his very short career he was one of the chief attractions of that attractive variety show, for the *Black Crook* in its later years was nothing more than a variety entertainment; and when, so soon after the close of his engagement here, the news of his death came from Boston, few of the established favorites of many years have been so sincerely mourned as was this unfortunate little James G. Speaight.

Scarcely larger than the violin he carried, dressed in a bright court suit of blue satin, with powdered wig and silken hose and buckled shoes, like a prince in a fairy tale, he seemed the slightest mite of a performer who ever stood behind the foot-lights. His hands were scarcely big enough to grasp his instrument; his arms and his legs were not so thick as his bow; a bit of rosin thrown at him would have knocked him down; and he could have been packed away comfortably in the case of his own fiddle. As a musician he certainly was phenomenal. It was said of him that when only four years of age, and after a single hearing, he could play by ear the most difficult and complicated of musical compositions, and that he could remember an air as soon as he could utter an articulate sound. Before he was five years old he was sole performer at concerts given under his father's management in some of the provincial towns of England; and when he first appeared in this country he not only played solos upon his violin, displaying decided genius and technical skill, but he conducted the large orchestra standing on a pile of music-books in the chair of the leader, that he might be seen of the musicians he led.

The grace and ease of the little artist, his enthusiasm and vivacity, could not fail to interest and amuse his audiences, while at the same time it saddened the most thoughtful of them, who realized how unnatural and how cruel to the child the whole proceeding must of necessity be. That he was passionately fond of his art there could be no doubt, or that he lived only in and for it, and in the excitement and applause his public appearances brought him; but that his indulgence of his passion without proper restraint was the cause of the snapping of the strings of his little life, and of the wreck of what might have been a brilliant professional career, was plainly manifest to every physician, and to every mother who saw and heard and pitied him.

Until within a very few months of his death he played only by ear. When he began to learn his notes, and to comprehend the immensity of music as a science, and the magnificent future it promised him, his devotion to study, his ambition, and his own active mind were more than his feeble frame could endure, and his brief candle was suddenly extinguished. At the close of this run of the *Black Crook*, December 6, 1873, he was taken to Boston, where he played in the *Naiad Queen*, and led the orchestra of the Boston Theatre until the night of the 11th of January, 1874. After the *matinée* and evening performance of that date he was heard by his father to murmur in his troubled sleep, "O God, can you make room for a little fellow like me?" and he was found dead by his father at daybreak. With no sins of his own to answer for, surely the prayer was heard; and the coming of that little child was not forbidden.

The few musical prodigies who have succeeded Master Speaight in this country have been blessed, happily, with stronger constitutions or with wiser guardians; and Munrico Dengremont, Josef Hofman, and Otto Hegner, so far at least, have found the rest they need before it is too late. The little Dengremont, a violinist, began his professional life at the age of eight, and in 1875. He came of musical people, he had studied hard, and as a phenomenon he was very successful. He first appeared in New York in 1881, when he was fourteen years of age, but he seems to have produced nothing, and to have done nothing since he went back to Europe some years ago.

The infant musician who of late years attracted the greatest attention in this country, next to the "Child Violinist" noticed in the opening of this chapter, was unquestionably Josef Hofman; and he appealed particularly to a class of the community so high in the social scale, according to its own ideas, that it repudiated Niblo's Garden and the *Black Crook* as vulgar. It never heard of little Speaight until it heard of his death, and it knows nothing of him now, perhaps, except as the mythical hero of charming and sympathetic poems written in his memory by Thomas Bailey Aldrich and Austin Dobson.

Hofman was born in Cracow, in 1877. His mother was an opera-singer, his father a teacher of music. The child had a piano of his own before he was five years of age, and in six months he had acquired the principles of musical composition, and had written an original mazourka. He made his first public appearance at a charity concert when he was six; at eight he played at a public concert at Berlin; and at ten he was drawing enormous crowds to the largest theatre in New York. He was the subject of more attention and of more newspaper notice, perhaps, than any musical child who ever lived. Saint-Saëns, the French composer, is said to have declared that he had nothing more to learn in music, that everything in him was music; and Rubinstein is said to have pronounced him the greatest wonder of the present age. All of this would have turned a bigger head than his; but notwithstanding his remarkable genius he was always a boy, who found relief in toy steamers and in tin soldiers; and his parents were sensible enough and humane enough to shut up his piano, and to sacrifice their ambition for the good of their son. He is devoting his youth to natural study, and his public career is still before him.

The little Hegner, the latest prodigy, made his first appearance in America in 1889, when he was twelve years of age; and he, too, came of a musical family. Like the Hofman infant, the piano is his instrument, and those who know music speak enthusiastically of his "phrasing," of his "interpretations," of his "striking perceptions of musical form," and the like. All of these children have been compared with Mozart and Liszt, who are, no doubt, innocently responsible for most of the infant musical wonders who have been born since they themselves began, as babies, to perform marvels. There has been but one Mozart, and but one Liszt; and the yet unwritten history of their lives will show whether these lads of the present would not have grown up to be greater artists and happier men if they had in their youth played football instead of fiddles, and had paid more attention to muscle than to music.

Between the musical wonder and the theatrical wonder there is this distinction: the baby musician never plays baby tunes, the infant actor almost always plays child's parts. Little Cordelia Howard, as Eva, many years ago, and Elsie Leslie and Thomas Russell, alternating in the character of Little Lord Fauntleroy last season, were doing very remarkable things in a charmingly natural way; but if they had attempted to play Macbeth and Lady Macbeth they would only have done what the

musical prodigies are doing when they attempt
Mendelssohn's D Minor Concerto or a mazourka by
Chopin. The little actors are certainly the more
rational, the more tolerable, and the more patiently
to be endured.

Of the class of prodigies represented by Mr. and
Mrs. Stratton ("Tom Thumb" and Lavinia Warren),
"Major" Stevens, "Commodore" Nutt, "Blind Tom,"
"Japanese Tommy," and the "Two-headed
Nightingale," all of whom were publicly exhibited
in their childhood here, it is hardly necessary to
speak. They were certainly Infant Phenomena, but
neither as infants nor as phenomena do they come
within the proper scope of the present chapter; and
they occupy the same position in regard to the
drama that the armless youth who cuts paper
pictures with his toes occupies in regard to pictorial
art.

In no case is the Infant Phenomenon upon the stage-
-thespian, terpsichorean, harmonical, gymnastic, or
abnormal--to be encouraged or admired. How much
of a nuisance the average prodigy is to his
audiences all habitual theatre-goers can tell; how
much of a nuisance he is to his fellow-players
Nicholas Nickleby has effectively shown; and what
a bitter burden he is likely to become to himself, his
own experience--if he lives to have experience--will
certainly prove. Loved by the gods--of the gallery--
the Phenomenon (happily for the Phenomenon,
perhaps, certainly happily for his profession) dies,
as a rule, young.

He does not educate the masses; he does not

advance art; he does nothing which it is the high aim of the legitimate actor to do; he does not even amuse. He merely displays precocity that is likely to sap his very life; he probably supports a family at an age when he needs all of the protection and support that can be given him; and, if he does not meet a premature death, he rarely, very rarely, fulfils anything like the promise of his youth.

The career of Master Betty, the "Infant Roscius," of the early part of this century, and unquestionably the most remarkable and successful Phenomenon in the whole history of the stage, is ample proof of this. Born in England, in 1791, he made his theatrical *début* in Dublin in 1803, and he at once sprang into a popularity, there and wherever he appeared, which seemed to know no limits.

The excitement he created was marvellous. People were crushed in their efforts to enter the theatres in which he played. The receipts at the box-offices were considered fabulous in those days. His own fortune was made in a single season. Lords and ladies, and peers of the realm, were among his enthusiastic admirers. Royal dukes were proud to call him friend, and the Prince of Wales entertained him regally at Carlton House. He was pronounced greater than Garrick himself in Garrick's own parts; he was petted and praised, and almost idolized, by an entire country; and even Parliament itself, on a motion made by Mr. Pitt, adjourned to see the "Infant Roscius" play Hamlet at Drury Lane; than which no higher compliment could have been paid by England to mortal man!

This mania over the boy actor continued for two or
three seasons, when his popularity by degrees
decreased, and he retired from the stage to enter the
University of Cambridge. In 1812, however, he
returned to the profession a young man of twenty-
one, but his prestige was gone. He did not draw in
London; in the provinces he was regarded as
nothing but a fair stock actor; and when he was a
little more than thirty years of age he retired entirely
into private life. He died in London, August 24,
1874, a man of eighty-three, having outlived his
glory by at least fifty years. If such was the lot of
the most marvellous of prodigies, what better fate
can the managers of the lesser juvenile stars expect
for their child wonders?

The career of Macready, a contemporary of Master
Betty's during his later efforts, as compared with
that of the Phenomenon, shows in a marked degree
the difference between the natural and the forced
systems of dramatic education. Macready, after
years of careful, conscientious study and training,
went upon the stage a young man, but one mature in
experience. By hard work he made his way up to
the top of the ladder of professional fame, and he
died full of years, honored as the most finished
actor of his day in his own land. Betty, at whom as a
child he had wondered, and whom as a young man
he had supported, surviving him a month or two,
was carried to his grave by a few personal friends,
almost unnoticed by the world who at one time had
worshipped his genius, but to whom for half a
century he had been absolutely dead. Macready, a
fixed star, shining brightly and bravely, gave a
lasting, steady, truthful light. Betty, streaming like a

meteor in the troubled air, eclipsing for a moment all of the planets in his course, plunged into a sea of oblivion and left only a ripple behind.

Two precocious youths, whose careers upon the American stage were not unlike that of Master Betty in England, were Master Payne and Master Burke. John Howard Payne is remembered now as the author of "Home Sweet Home"; he is almost forgotten as the writer of the tragedy of *Brutus* and some sixty other plays; and he is forgotten entirely as a very successful child actor in the highest range of parts. He made his *début* as Young Norval in *Douglas* at the Park Theatre, New York, in 1809, when he was but seventeen years of age. He was called "the favorite child of Thespis," and his performance was declared to be exquisite, one enthusiastic gentleman giving fifty dollars for a single ticket at his benefit in Baltimore. He supported Miss O'Neill in the British provinces, and Mrs. Duff in New York; but as soon as he was billed as *Mister* Payne, not *Master* Payne, his popularity ceased, and, except as a playwright, the stage knew him no more.

Master Burke was a more unusual wonder, for he was a musical as well as a theatrical Phenomenon. Born in Ireland, Thomas Burke made his *début* in Cork as Tom Thumb, when he was five years of age. He made his first appearance in America at the Park Theatre, New York, in 1830, before he was twelve. Mr. Ireland preserves a list of characters he played, which includes Richard III., Shylock, Norval, Sir Abel Handy, Sir Giles Overreach, and Doctor Pangloss. He also led the orchestra in operatic overtures, played violin solos, and sung humorous songs; and "as a prodigy, both in music and the drama," Mr. Ireland believes that "he has been unapproached by any child who has trodden the American stage." As a man, he was considered one of the most perfect violinists of his time, and he was last heard here in public at the concerts of Jenny Lind, Jullien, and Thalberg, many years ago.

The cynical remark of Richard to the young Prince of Wales that "so wise so young, they say, do ne'er live long," does not always apply to stage children. The Batemans, Miss Mary McVicker, Miss Matilda Heron, Miss Clara Fisher, Miss Jean Margaret Davenport (from whose early career Dickens is believed to have drawn the character of Miss Crummles), and other juvenile wonders, lived to achieve more enduring greatness as men and women than was ever thrust upon them in their childish days--while many of the present veterans in the profession were on the stage as actors before they were old enough to read or write. Miss Fanny Davenport and Miss Susan Denin made their dramatic *débuts* as children in *The Stranger*, *Pizarro*, *Metamora*, or other of the standard plays of their youth; Mr. Jefferson, at the age of six, engaged in a stage combat with broadswords with one Master Titus, at the Park Theatre, for the benefit of the latter young gentleman; and Madame Ristori, carried upon the stage in a basket at the age of two months, was at the age of four years playing children's parts in her native Italy. Miss Lotta began her professional career a Phenomenon when eight years old; but Lotta, to be measured by no known dramatic rules, is an Infant Phenomenon still. Miss

Mary Taylor, than whom no lady in her maturity enjoyed greater popularity in New York, sang as a child in concerts, and even before she reached her teens was a great favorite in the choruses of the National Theatre on Church Street, New York; and there are to-day, among collectors of such things, rare prints, highly prized, of Miss Adelaide Phillips and of Miss Mary Gannon as child wonders; the latter young lady having been an actress before she was three years old.

Evidences of such early dramatic experiences might readily be multiplied; but a decided distinction should be made between the phenomenal young actor or actress who walks upon the stage in leading parts, a child Richard or an infant Richmond, and the youthful artist, born of dramatic parents, who, never attempting what is beyond his years or his station, plays Young York or Young Clarence to support his father, says his few lines, gets his little bit of applause, is not noticed by the critics, and goes home like a good child to his mother and to his bed. It is as natural for the child of an actor to go upon the stage as it is for the son of a sailor to follow the sea; but while the young mariner before the mast is taught the rudiments of his profession by the roughest of experiences and the hardest of knocks, the young Roscius too frequently is given command of his dramatic ship before he can box the dramatic compass, or can tell the difference in the nautical drama between *Black-eyed Susan* and *The Tempest*.

Miss Clara Fisher (Mrs. James G. Maeder) was regarded in her youth as a prodigy second only to

Master Betty; but, unlike Master Betty, she more than realized the best hopes of her early admirers, and lived to be considered one of the most perfect and finished actresses ever known to our stage. Born in England in 1811, she appeared in Drury Lane, London, the scene of Master Betty's earliest successes, when she was only six years of age, and at once she won the most decided triumphs. It was said of her that she clearly understood, even at that early age, her author and his meaning, entered thoroughly and enthusiastically into all of her parts, and displayed in every scene not only acuteness of intellect, but a temperament fully in unison with the profession of her choice. Cast in plays with actors of the regulation age and size, instead of being dwarfed by the contrast with them, she made the rest of the *dramatis personæ* appear entirely out of proportion, and carried away all of the honors. Her American *début* was made September 12, 1827, at the Park Theatre, New York. In the seventeenth year of her age she could scarcely rank among the Infant Phenomena, however, and she is only known in this country, where the rest of her professional life has been spent, as a leading lady, justly celebrated, but not wonderful, out of all whooping, as an Infant Roscia.

Mrs. Maeder comes of a theatrical race, and one which seems to mature early. Her sister, Jane Marchant Fisher, the good old Mrs. Vernon of Wallack's, went upon the stage in London a child of ten; Frederick G. Maeder, her son, made his first appearance at the age of eighteen; and Alexina Fisher (Mrs. A. F. Baker) and Oceana Fisher, daughters of Palmer Fisher, and members of the same family, played here as children half a century ago.

The most remarkable and most successful of the Infant Phenomena of modern times in America have been the Bateman Children, the Marsh Juvenile Troupe, and the Boone and the Holman Children. On the 10th of December, 1849, E. A. Marshall, manager of the Broadway Theatre, introduced on the boards of that house, for the first time to New York audiences, Kate and Ellen Bateman, whose united ages were not ten years. Kate made her *début* as Richmond, and Ellen, the younger, as Richard, in scenes from Shakspere's *Richard III.* The announcement of the coming of the infantile Thespians was not favorably received by the regular attendants of the Broadway; the appearance of prodigies of any kind being a departure from the ways of that traditional home of the legitimate drama, and there was a prejudice formed against these young stars which nothing but the absolute cleverness of their performances was able to overcome. After Mr. Hackett as Falstaff, and Miss Cushman as Lady Macbeth, it was scarcely natural that unknown children in the same and kindred parts should satisfy the critical audiences of the Old Broadway. The popularity of the Batemans, however, was quickly established; those who came to scoff on the first night returned to praise; the whole town, young and old, petted and applauded the children; while still the wonder grew, during the single week of their engagement, how the two small heads could carry all they knew. It seemed incredible that an infant of four years like Ellen Bateman could present anything approaching an embodiment of such characters as Shylock, Richard, or Lady Macbeth; or that a child of six, as was Kate at that time, should be able to play Richmond, Portia, or the Thane with the correctness of elocution, the spirit, and the proper comprehension of the language and the business which she displayed. The simple task of committing to memory the text of so many parts was in itself a marvellous effort for children of their tender age, but to be able to speak these lines as set down for them with correct emphasis and gesture, and with every appearance of a thorough conception of the character sustained, as the little Batemans are said to have done, certainly warranted all the praise that was bestowed upon them. Every fresh character they undertook was a surprise, and was considered more clever than any that had preceded it. Lady Macbeth was, perhaps, the most successful of Ellen's assumptions, while Kate read Portia with amazing skill and propriety; her delivery of the familiar lines was finished, and her carriage throughout was that of an experienced artist.

After appearing in Boston, Baltimore, Philadelphia, and other American cities, the Bateman Children were taken to England by P. T. Barnum, in the summer of 1851, making their first appearance there at the St. James's Theatre, London, on the 23d August, as *The Young Couple*, and meeting with decided success. They returned to the Old Broadway November 15, 1852, and opened in a comedietta entitled *Her Royal Highness*, written expressly for them. They were quite as popular here as when they first appeared, and before they left New York Mayor Kingsland, "on behalf of a committee of leading citizens," presented to each of the children a tiny gold watch.

In 1856, no longer juveniles, though still most acute, voluble, and full of grace, they retired from the stage. Miss Kate Bateman returned to it, however, in a few years, a young lady, and an actress of more than ordinary merit. Even if she had not since then made for herself, both in this country and in England, a reputation as one of the strongest tragic and melodramatic artists on the English-speaking stage, the story of her early career as told here is worthy of a place in dramatic history because of the precocious excellence of her acting as a child, and of the wonderful success which she everywhere won. She was a Phenomenon among Phenomena in this respect, that she grew and advanced in her profession as she grew in stature and advanced in years--one of the very few of the infant prodigies who, in later life, became an ornament to the stage.

On the 10th of December, 1855, precisely six years after the first appearance of the Bateman Children at the Broadway Theatre, the Marsh Juvenile Troupe made their first appearance here at the same house, and made, also, a very favorable impression even upon critics not predisposed to be attracted by any exhibition of prodigies. In their acting was a perceptible absence of that familiar, parrot-like, mechanical repetition of unfamiliar words, and of those studied and artificial attitudes so painfully marked in juvenile players generally. Their impersonations were spirited and exact, and evinced unusual mental aptitude and training, their audiences being sometimes startled by the extraordinary precocity with which some of the leading parts were filled. Their initial performance consisted of *Beauty and the Beast*, Miss Louisa Marsh representing the Beast, while little Mary Marsh, as Beauty, pleasantly filled all of the personal and mental requirements of that *rôle*. *Beauty and the Beast* was followed by *The Wandering Minstrel*, Master George H. Marsh playing Jem Baggs, "with the popular, doleful, pathetic, sympathetic, lamentable history of 'Villikins and his Dinah.'" These were supplemented later, during the Marshes' engagement, with *The Rivals*--Mr. Blake as Sir Anthony, Madame Ponisi as Julia--or with *A Morning Call*, Madame Ponisi playing Mrs. Chillington, and Augustus A. Fenno Sir Edward; the Juveniles, although attractive, being scarcely successful in filling the house by their sole exertions.

The Marsh Children, although generally announced by that name on the bills, were not members of one family, nor were they Marshes. George and Mary, brother and sister, and both of them said to have been less than eight years of age when they came here first, were in private life Master and Miss Guerineau--while the other leading lady, Louisa Marsh, was properly Miss McLaughlin. The entire company was composed of children. As they died-- and the mortality among them was remarkable--or as they grew too large for the troupe, their places were filled by other precocious infants, engaged by their clever manager in his strollings from town to town. Among the members of the company at different times were Miss Ada Webb, Miss Fanny

Berkley, Miss Ada and Miss Minnie Monk, and
Louis Aldrich, all of whom, if not great,
subsequently, in their profession, are still not
unknown to fame. Unlike the Batemans, however,
none of the Marsh Juveniles ever became stars of
more than common magnitude, and none of them
are shining very brilliantly on the stage to-day.
George Marsh, the low comedian, was very clever
in his way, although not original in his
impersonations. His powers of imitation were
marvellous, and his Toodles, a miniature copy of
Burton's Toodles, in which all of the business and
many of the gags--even to the profanity at the
mention of Thompson--were retained, was almost
as funny in its uproariousness as was Burton's
Toodles itself, and certainly better than many of the
imitations that have been seen since Burton's day.
Little Mary Marsh was an uncommonly attractive
child, bright-eyed, graceful, fresh, and fair. The boy
between eight and fifteen in her audiences who did
not succumb to her loveliness was only fit for
treason, stratagem, and spoils. Her name was to be
found written in some copy-book, her face sketched
in some drawing-book in the male department of
every school in New York, and in the average
schoolboy's mind she was associated in some
romantic way with all of the good and beautiful
women of his history or his mythology; she
inhabited all the salubrious and balmy isles in his
geography; she was dreamed of in his philosophy;
and one particular lad, who is now more than old
enough to pay the school bills of boys of his own,
when asked, in a chemistry class, by the master,
"What is the symbol and equivalent of potassium?"
answered, absently, but without hesitation, "Mary

Marsh!"

The passion the child inspired in the breasts of her adorers was a pure one, and, except in the neglect of a prosy lesson or two, it did no harm. Her memory is still kept green in the hearts of many practical men of to-day, who unblushingly confess to a filling of their boyish eyes and a quivering of their boyish lips when the sad story of her untimely and dreadful death was told here. While playing in one of the Southern cities, her dress took fire from the footlights and she was fatally burned, living but an hour or two after the accident occurred.

On the 3d of August, 1857, the Marshes played *Black-eyed Susan* at Laura Keene's Theatre here, followed by *The Toodles*. From thc bill of this, their opening night, the following casts are copied:

BLACK-EYED SUSAN.

William Miss Louisa Marsh. Gnatbrain Master George H. Marsh. Tom Bowling Master Alfred (Stewart). Admiral Master Waldo (Todd). Dolly Mayflower Miss Carrie (Todd). Black-eyed Susan Miss Mary Marsh.

TOODLES.

Timothy Toodles Master George H. Marsh. George Acorn Miss Louisa Marsh. Tabitha Toodles Miss Mary Marsh.

This was probably the last season of the Marsh Juveniles in New York, and since their exit no startling troupe of Phenomena have appeared here. The Boone and the Holman Children were clever, but not so successful as the Marshes. The Worrell Sisters were popular, but, although young girls, they were in their teens, and scarcely came under the head of infant players. They made their New York *début* at Wood's Theatre, 514 Broadway, afterwards the Theatre Comique, under the management of George Wood, in a burletta called *The Elves*, April 30, 1866, Miss Sophie Worrell, the eldest of the three sisters, being at that time fully eighteen years of age.

Among the occasional companies of children who have appeared in New York were "The Mexican Juvenile Troupe." They occupied Mr. Daly's Fifth Avenue Theatre during the summer season of 1875, remaining two weeks, and appearing at the Lyceum Theatre, on Fourteenth Street, from the 1st to the 13th of November in the same year. Their performances were conducted in the Spanish language, and their specialty was opera-bouffe. They were well trained in voice and action, but the music in their childish treble was weak; and, personally, the troupe ran to legs and arms and hands and feet, and the general angular and awkward undevelopment characteristic of their age and size. The bit of a *prima donna* who sang La Grand Duchesse and La Belle Hélène in the titular parts, and who was known to fame as Signorina Carmen Unda y Moron, was made up carefully after Tostée, whom, in certain actions and gestures and expression of face, she much resembled. She displayed all of the vim and *abandon* and *chic* of the veteran actress, and tossed her head, and switched her train, and ogled and leered, and capered like the very Tostée herself, as seen through the reverse of an opera-glass. The child acted with spirit, or something that was like it, and seemed to have a morbid enjoyment and comprehension of the indelicate parts she played. The spectacle was far from being a pleasant one, and probably shocked more persons than it amused. Little Carmen was certainly not more than eight years old, and barely as tall as the table in her stage parlor, while none of the company reached in height the backs of the chairs of ordinary size with which, in strange incongruity, the stage of the Lyceum was always set.

During the past fifteen or twenty years there have appeared upon the New York stage, generally unheralded, several little actors and actresses who have shown decided ability for the profession, while claiming no phenomenal talent, and in whom certainly there seemed to be fair promise of a brilliant future. Among these have been little Minnie Maddern, who appeared at the French Theatre on Fourteenth Street, May 30, 1870, as Sibyl Carew, in Tom Taylor's *Sheep in Wolf's Clothing*, supporting Miss Carlotta Leclercq as Anne. Her knowledge of stage business, her general carriage, and the careful delivery of her lines throughout the play were remarkable for a child of her years; and hers was considered one of the most satisfactory representations in the piece. The pleasant reputation she made there was sustained at Booth's Theatre in the month of May, 1874, when she played Arthur in *King John*, with Junius Brutus Booth, Jr., in the titular part, Mrs. Agnes Booth as

Constance, and John McCullough as the Bastard--a
good cast. A more pretentious Arthur--an older, not
a better one--was that of Master Percy Roselle, who
played it in one act of *King John* at a *matinée*
benefit given to Miss Matilda Heron, January 17,
1872.

Miss Jennie Yeamans was *almost* a Phenomenon,
although, fortunately for herself, she was never
subjected by her managers to the forcing process.
As Joseph in a burlesque of *Richelieu*, at the
Olympic, in February, 1871, she was very good,
second only to George Fox as the Cardinal-Duke,
whom, with a piece of chalk, she assisted in
drawing the awful circle of the Tammany Ring
around the form of Miss Lillie Eldridge as Julie.
The solemnity of the entire performance on the
child's part, her wonderful command of her features,
and her display of a dry, apparently unconscious
humor, all in the true spirit of burlesque, were
delightful to contemplate. She was equally good
and amusing in a part of an entirely different nature,
Notah, the Little Pappoose, in Augustin Daly's
Horizon, a little later in the same season at the same
house. Representing an Indian child who had no
knowledge of the English tongue, and who united to
the natural mischievousness of childhood all of the
untamed viciousness of the Indian nature, she was
captured on the plains by the Hon. Sundown Bowse
(G. L. Fox), and she made that gentleman's stage
existence more than a burden to him through
several acts. When Charles Fisher played Falstaff at
the Fifth Avenue Theatre she was an excellent
William Page.

Miss Mabel Leonard, apparently some five years old, supported H. J. Montague at Wallack's Theatre in the month of October, 1874, when the *Romance of a Poor Young Man* was produced, playing with a good deal of skill a little Breton peasant girl. The same young lady and Bijou Heron were the children in Miss Morris's version of *East Lynne*, called *Miss Multon*, at the Union Square Theatre in November, 1876. Their judicious training, and the careful acting of their not unimportant parts, added much to the general completeness of the drama, and will be still vividly remembered by all now living who were play-goers years ago.

Of all the children who have appeared upon the stage during the past twenty years, Bijou Heron was one of the brightest and most promising. In face refined, intelligent, and attractive, in voice pleasant and sympathetic, in figure neat, graceful, and *petite* even for her years, she had all the personal requirements of success in her profession, combined with careful training, quick comprehension, tact, intelligence, and love for her art. As the only child, and as the hope and idol of a once favorite actress, whose popularity was of so comparatively recent a date that she had not passed out of the memory of the theatre-goers of her daughter's time, she was kindly and affectionately received in New York for Matilda Heron's sake, even before she had won for herself, and by her own exertions, so many friends here.

After long preparation she made her first appearance on any stage at Daly's Fifth Avenue Theatre, Twenty-eighth Street, on April 14, 1874, in

a play entitled *Monsieur Alphonse*, from the French
of the younger Dumas, by Mr. Daly, and first
presented that evening in this country. It was
probably one of the most thoroughly successful
débuts witnessed here in many years. Aside from
the shyness and constraint so natural to the
débutante, and without which no true actor ever
stepped for the first time before a critical public, she
bore herself naturally, simply, and with charming
grace. The part is long and difficult, not one of the
commonplace, childish *rôles* usually intrusted to
infant players, nor one of the high tragedy star *rôles*
sometimes inflicted upon juvenile prodigies, but a
bit of leading juvenile business requiring more than
ordinary intelligence and skill upon the part of its
representative. Many actresses who have been years
upon the stage, and who are considered beyond the
average in their playing, would have played it with
less appreciation and success.

Of the juvenile actors of the present time something
has already been said. As a rule they belong to the
legitimate branches of the profession, and they are
as rational, perhaps, as is the drummer-boy of the
army, the elevator-boy of society, or the cash-boy of
trade. Alice in Wonderland adorns a charming tale,
Prince and Pauper and Little Lord Fauntleroy point
a pretty moral, even Editha's Burglar may have his
uses; but, take them as a whole, it is a difficult
matter to determine the exact position of the Infant
Phenomena upon the stage. They occupy, perhaps,
the neutral ground between the amateurs and the
monstrosities, without belonging to either class, or
to art. As professional performers, although in
embryo, they cannot share exemption from the

severe tests of criticism with those who only play at being players; and as human beings, although undeveloped, they cannot be judged as leniently as are the learnèd pigs and the trained monkeys from whom some of Mr. Darwin's disciples might believe them to be evolved. The public demands them, however, and dramatists make them; therefore let them pass for stars!

ACT V.

A CENTURY OF AMERICAN HAMLETS.

A CENTURY OF AMERICAN HAMLETS.

"So please you, something touching the Lord Hamlet." *Hamlet*, Act i. Sc. 3.

Hamlet, in his wholesome advice to the players, in his command to the garrulous old gentleman who would have been his father-in-law had Hamlet been a low comedy instead of a high tragedy part, that the players be well bestowed, and in his bold assertion that the play's the thing, showed plainly how great was his interest in the drama, and how keen his appreciation of what the Profession ought to be. Hamlet has done much for the players, but the players have cruelly wronged Hamlet. They have mouthed him, and strutted him, and bellowed him, have sawn him in the air with their hands, and have torn his passions to tatters, till it were better for Hamlet often that the town-crier himself had spoken his lines. A very few of our tragedians of the city have had enough respect for the character of Hamlet to let him alone. Others have done full justice to Hamlet, and as Hamlet have reflected credit upon Hamlet and upon themselves; but there have been players that I have seen play, and heard others praise, and that highly, who, not to speak it profanely, having neither the accent of Christians nor the gait of Christian, pagan, or man, have made nights and *matinées* hideous with the part, and have done murder most foul to Hamlet.

There can be no question that New York is the dramatic metropolis of the United States--and despite the absence of anything like State aid--as certainly as Paris is the capital of France, and as surely as London is the centre of Great Britain. A New York success is of as much importance to the new play and to the young player as is the crown of the Academy to the new book, or the degree to the young doctor; and a history of *Hamlet* in New York, therefore, is virtually a history of *Hamlet* in America.

The tragedy has been played here during the last century and a quarter in many languages, by actors of all ages and of both sexes, in blond wigs and in natural black hair, with elaborate scenery and with no scenery at all, by almost every tragedian in the country, and on the stage of almost every theatre in the city with the exception of Wallack's last theatre, now Palmer's. It has been burlesqued, and sung as an opera; and its representatives have been good, bad, and very, very indifferent. So much is there to be said about *Hamlet* in New York that the great difficulty in preparing this sketch of its career is the proper and natural selection of what not to say.

Hamlet was first presented in the city of New York on the evening of the 26th of November, 1761, and at the "New Theatre in Chappel Street"--now Beekman Street--near Nassau, the younger Lewis Hallam, the original Hamlet in America (at Philadelphia, in the autumn of 1759), playing the titular part. Hallam was a versatile actor, who was

on the stage in this country for over fifty years, and
always popular. Concerning his Hamlet very little is
now known, except the curious statement in the
Memoirs of Alexander Graydon, published in 1811,
that Hallam once ventured to appear as Hamlet in
London--"and was endured!" He was the
acknowledged leading tragedian of the New York
stage until his retirement in 1806, and he is known
to have played Hamlet as late as 1797, when he
must have been close upon sixty years of age. Mr.
Ireland is of the impression that John Hodgkinson, a
contemporary of Hallam's, who appeared as Hamlet
in Charleston, South Carolina, early in the present
century, conceded Hallam's rights to the character
in the metropolis, and never attempted it here.

The first Hamlet in New York in point of quality,
and perhaps the second in point of time, was that of
Thomas Abthorpe Cooper, who played the part at
the John Street Theatre on the 22d of November,
1797, although Mr. Ireland believes that he was
preceded by Mr. Moreton at the theatre on
Greenwich Street, in the summer of the same year,
as he had played the Ghost to Moreton's Hamlet in
Baltimore a short time before. William Dunlap
speaks in the highest terms of Cooper's Hamlet, and
John Bernard ranks it with the Hamlet of John
Philip Kemble himself.

James Fennell, a brilliant but uncertain English
actor, who came to America in 1794, was the next
Hamlet worthy of note to appear in New York. He
was at the John Street Theatre as early as 1797, but
he does not seem to have undertaken the character
of the Dane until 1806, when he was at the Park for

a few nights. He was an eccentric person, who
figures in all of the dramatic memoirs of his time,
and who published in 1841 a very remarkable book,
called an *Apology* for his own life. Educated for the
Church, he became in turn--and nothing long--an
actor in the provinces of England, a teacher of
declamation in Paris, a writer for the press in
London, and a salt-maker, a bridge-builder, a
lecturer, an editor, a school-master, and again and
again an actor in America. John Bernard speaks of
him as that "whirligig-weathercock-fellow Fennell,"
and as "the maddest madman I ever knew." He was
excellent as Othello and Iago, and, according to Mr.
Ireland, "beyond all competition as Zanga," but
concerning his Hamlet history is silent.

John Howard Payne enjoys the distinction of being
the first American Hamlet who was born in
America, and he had been born but seventeen years
when he played Hamlet at the Park Theatre in May,
1809. Two years later, on the 5th of April, 1811, he
introduced the tragedy to Albany audiences, and his
Hamlet, naturally, was as immature and as amateur
as it was premature.

Other juvenile tragedians followed Master Payne
upon the stage when they should have been in bed,
notably Master George F. Smith, who played
Hamlet at the Park Theatre on the 28th of March,
1822, and, very notably, Master Joseph Burke, who
played in Dublin in 1824, when he was five years
old, and who was recognized as a star in *Hamlet* in
the United States when he was twelve.

But to leave the pygmies and return to the giants.

Play-goers in New York between the years 1810 and 1821 were blessed, as play-goers have never been blessed before, in being able to enjoy and to compare the performances of three of the greatest actors it has ever been the lot of any single pair of eyes to see or of any single pair of ears to hear: to wit, Cooke, Kean, and Booth. George Frederick Cooke arrived in America in 1810, and remained here until his death in 1812. Setting at defiance all the laws of nature, society, and art, he was in nothing more remarkable than in the fact that in the whole history of the drama in this country he is the only really great tragedian, old or young, who never attempted to play Hamlet here. His diary records his failure in the part in London years before; and Leigh Hunt, who praises him highly in other lines, says that he could willingly spare the recollection of his Hamlet, and that "the most accomplished character on the stage he converted into an unpolished, obstinate, sarcastic madman."

Edmund Kean first played Hamlet in New York in the month of December, 1820, Junius Brutus Booth in the October of the following year. Concerning these men and their rivalry volumes have been written; each had his enthusiastic admirers, and the Hamlet of each has become a matter of history. That Kean believed in his own Hamlet in his younger days there can be no question now, and he gave to it the closest study until the widow of Garrick induced him to alter his reading of the "closet scene," and to adopt the manner of her band; an innovation which left him ever after dissatisfied with himself in that part of the tragedy. Hazlitt considered Kean's kissing of Ophelia's hand, in the famous scene between them in Act III., "the finest commentary that was ever made on Shakspere.... The manner in which Mr. Kean acted in the scene of the play before the King and Queen," he adds, "was the most daring of any, and the force and animation which he gave it cannot be too highly applauded. Its extreme boldness bordered 'on the verge of all we hate,' and the effect it produced was a test of the extraordinary powers of this extraordinary actor." The younger Booth, writing of the elder Kean, defends his father's foe in the following noble words: "The fact that Kean disliked to act Hamlet, and failed to satisfy his critics in that character, is no proof that his personation was false. If it was consistent with his conception, and that conception was intelligible, as it must have been, it was true. What right have I, whose temperament and mode of thinking are dissimilar to yours, to denounce your exposition of such a puzzle as Hamlet? He is the epitome of mankind, not an individual: a sort of magic mirror in which all men and all women see the reflex of themselves, and therefore has his story always been, is still, and will ever be the most popular of stage tragedies."

That Edwin Booth should not have written concerning the Hamlet of his father in the same charming vein is greatly to be regretted. There are men still living who recollect the elder Booth in the part--he played it for the last time in New York in 1843--and to these it is one of the most delightful of memories. Thomas R. Gould, writing in 1868, sums up as follows his own ideas of the Hamlet of this great man: "The total impression left by his impersonation at the time of its occurrence, and

which still abides, was that of a spiritual
melancholy, at once acute and profound. This
quality colored his tenderest feeling and his airiest
fancy. You felt its presence even when he was off
the stage."

This famous decade of the New York stage saw
other great actors and other great Hamlets, some of
whom in point of time preceded Kean and Booth.
Joseph George Holman played Hamlet at the Park
Theatre in September, 1812, James William
Wallack, on the same stage, in September, 1818,
Robert Campbell Maywood in 1819, John Jay
Adams in 1822, William Augustus Conway in
1824, Thomas Hamblin in 1825, and last, but not
least, William Charles Macready in October, 1826.

Of the Hamlet of John R. Duff there is, strange to
say, no record in New York, although he played
here occasionally between the years 1814 and 1827.
He was very popular in Boston and Philadelphia,
and a writer in the Boston *Centinel*, in the autumn
of 1810, does "not hesitate to say, that in some of
the scenes [of *Hamlet*], and those of no ordinary
grade of difficulty, he has never been excelled on
the Boston boards." His wife is still considered by
certain old play-goers to have been the best Ophelia
ever seen in the United States, and no account of
the tragedy in this country can be complete without
mention of her name. As Ophelia, in New York and
elsewhere, she supported the elder Booth, the elder
Kean, the elder Conway, Cooper, Payne, Wallack,
and other stars; and Mr. Booth wrote to George
Holland in 1836 that he considered her "the greatest
actress in the world."

Mr. Macready was the first of a trio of remarkable Hamlets who came to this country from England at about the same period. Charles Kean was the second, in 1830, Charles Kemble the third, in 1832. Of Macready's Hamlet he says himself, in his *Reminiscences*: "The thought and practice I have through my professional career devoted to it, made it in my own judgment and in those [*sic*] of critics whom I had most reason to fear and respect, one of the most finished, though not the most popular, in my *repertoire*."

In Cole's *Biography of Charles Kean*, inspired by its subject and written under his direction, if not at his dictation, is the following account of his first attempt at Hamlet: "The new Hamlet was received with enthusiasm. From his entrance to the close of the performance the applause was unanimous and incessant. The celebrated 'Is it the King?' in the third act, produced an electrical effect. To use a favorite expression of his father's, 'The pit rose at him.'"

Concerning the Hamlet of Charles Kemble, his daughter wrote, in 1832: "I have acted Ophelia three times with my father, and each time in that beautiful scene where his madness and his love gush forth together, like a torrent swollen with storms that bears a thousand blossoms on its turbid waters, I have experienced such deep emotion as hardly to be able to speak.... Now the great beauty of all my father's performances, but particularly of Hamlet, is a wonderful accuracy in the detail of the character which he represents," etc.

All of this would seem to be *ex parte* evidence, but it is interesting nevertheless; and neither Mr. Macready, Mr. Kean, nor Miss Kemble, perhaps, was very far astray. On the other hand, George Henry Lewes (*On Actors and the Art of Acting*) says that "Macready's Hamlet was, in his opinion, bad, due allowance being made for the intelligence it displayed. He was lachrymose and fretful; too fond of a cambric pocket-handkerchief to be really effective.... It was 'a thing of shreds and patches,' not a whole." The flourishing of this handkerchief just before the play scene gave great offence to Forrest, who had the bad taste to hiss it in Edinburgh; and thus began the wretched feud which nearly convulsed two continents, and ended in bloodshed at Astor Place, New York.

Confessing that the elder Kean could not have surpassed the younger in certain melodramatic parts, Lewes adds that it was never an intellectual treat to see him (Charles Kean) play any of Shakspere's heroes; and the author of *The Actor* says: "Charles Kean's Hamlet has many beauties, but he is physically disqualified to do justice to any character in tragedy.... Nature has given him a most unmelodious voice, the sound of which seems to flow rather through his nose than its appropriate organ, a face altogether unsuited to the character he attempts, and we doubt if she ever intended him for an actor." Apropos of Kean's difficulties in the utterance of certain of the consonants, particularly *m* and *n*, the London *Punch* acknowledged his antiquarian researches, and thanked him for having proved Shylock to be a vegetarian by his reading of the following lines:

"You take my life When you do take the *beans*
whereby I live!"

Macready described Charles Kemble as a first-rate
actor in second-rate parts, and said that "in Hamlet
he was Charles Kemble at his heaviest," while other
critics dismiss his Hamlet as "passable." Thus do
the doctors of criticism disagree.

It was said of Forrest, many years ago, that "his
Hamlet seemed like some philosophical Hercules
rather than the sad, unhappy youth of Denmark." If
this was true of him when first spoken, it was much
more true of him in his representation of the part
during the later years of his life, and as he is only
remembered by the large majority of the play-goers
of the present. Forrest was too great an artist to play
badly any part he ever undertook, but his Hamlet
certainly was the least pleasing of all his
Shaksperian *rôles*. Physically, he was altogether too
robust. His too, too solid flesh was bone and
muscle. The soul of Hamlet, as drawn by his
creator, and as conceived by every thorough
Shaksperian student since Shakspere's day, could
hardly have existed in a frame so magnificent as
that which nature had given Edwin Forrest. No
subtle mind, wily as was Hamlet's, whether it were
sound or unsound, was ever found in so sound a
body. Forrest, when he was young enough to play
Hamlet, never knew what nerves or indigestion
were. He gave to the part no little thought, and no
doubt he understood it thoroughly; but that it did
not suit him physically, and that he realized the fact,
seemed often manifest when he was playing it. He
presented the tragedy at Niblo's Garden in 1860,

Edwin Booth--at the Winter Garden--appearing in
the same part at the same time; and the contrast
between the powerful robustious figure, deep chest
tones, and somewhat ponderous action of the elder
actor, and the lithe, poetic, romantic, melancholy
rendition of the younger, was very marked.

Forrest first played Hamlet in New York at the Park
Theatre, in the month of October, 1829, when he
was but twenty-three years of age; and at his last
public appearance here, November 22, 1872, he
read portions of the tragedy at Steinway Hall. Mr.
Eddy, Mr. Studley, and other tragedians of Mr.
Forrest's "school of acting" were not more
satisfactory in the part of Hamlet than was Mr.
Forrest himself. John McCullough, however, a pupil
of Forrest's, and his leading man for a number of
years, met with more success. Although a native of
Ireland, his professional life was begun and almost
entirely spent in America, and he may be
considered a native Hamlet, to this manor born. His
voice and action in certain scenes where loud
declamation is demanded by the text were quite
after the manner of Forrest, but as a whole he
excelled his master in the part. He was free from
mannerisms, his figure was manly and striking, he
was neither too puny nor too burly, his sentiment
was not mawkish, nor was his honesty brutal.

George Vandenhoff made his first appearance in
America at the Park Theatre, New York, on the 21st
of September, 1842, in the character of Hamlet,
when Miss Sarah Hildreth, afterwards the wife of
Gen. Benjamin F. Butler, was the Ophelia. The
Polonius was Henry Placide, whom Mr.

Vandenhoff, in his *Leaves from an Actor's Note-Book*, called "the best Polonius and the best actor in his varied line in this country"; the Ghost was William Abbott, a superior actor in the higher range of parts; the Grave-digger was John Fisher, very popular and very able; the Horatio was Thomas Barry, who won for himself in later years no little distinction in New York and in Boston in the highest tragedy *rôles*; and the first Mrs. Thomas Barry, an actress of some ability, was Mr. Vandenhoff's Player Queen.

The Hamlet of Edward L. Davenport was never so popular as it should have been, nor was Mr. Davenport himself properly appreciated as an actor during the last years of his life. He was out of the fashion so long that until a far-sighted management engaged him to play the part of Brutus, during the famous run of *Julius Cæsar* at Booth's Theatre in 1875-76, he was only known to the younger generation of theatre-goers, when he was known at all, as Miss Fanny Davenport's father! That Mr. Davenport, at the close of his long career, should have been banished to the Grand Opera-house, and to Wood's Museum, in upper Broadway, is a stronger argument in favor of the alleged degeneracy of the drama in this country than is the unhealthy popularity of the current variety shows, and the emotional plays from the French.

The faithful band of Mr. Davenport's friends who followed him to the west side of the town, during his occasional visits to the metropolis, found nothing in his acting to wean them from their allegiance, while he made many new and enthusiastic friends among the gods of the gallery, those keen and appreciative critics whose verdict, although not always the general verdict, is ever, in an artistic way, the most valuable and pleasing to the actor. But galleries, alas! do not fill managers' pockets, nor do they lead the popular taste; and Mr. Davenport, at one time a universal favorite in New York with galleries, boxes, and pits, lived to find himself, through no fault of his own, and to the lasting discredit of metropolitan audiences, neglected and ignored.

Hamlet was not Mr. Davenport's greatest part, as it is not the greatest part of many of the popular Hamlets of the present; his Sir Giles Overreach, his Bill Sikes, his Brutus, and his William, in *Black-eyed Susan*, were as fine as his Hamlet, if not finer; nevertheless it was a singularly complete conception of the character--scholarly, finished, and profound. In his younger days he played the part many times, and with some of the "finest combinations of talent" which the records of the stage can show. On the 16th of October, 1856, at Burton's Theatre, New York, Mark Smith was the Polonius, Burton and Placide the Grave-diggers, Charles Fisher the Ghost, and Mrs. Davenport the Ophelia to his Hamlet--a combination of strength in male parts almost unequalled. At Niblo's Garden, in 1861, Mrs. Barrow was his Ophelia, William Wheatley his Laertes, Thomas Placide his First Grave-digger, James William Wallack, Jr., his Ghost, and Mrs. Wallack the Queen; and at the Academy of Music, on the 21st of January, 1871, he played one act of *Hamlet* to the Ophelia of Miss Agnes Ethel, on the occasion of the famous Holland

Benefit, when the audience, as large as the great house would hold, was the only audience to which Mr. Davenport played Hamlet in many years that was at all worthy of the actor or his part. Miss Ethel was a perfect picture of the most beautiful Ophelia. It was her first attempt at anything like a legitimate tragedy part, and was decidedly successful.

The several engagements of Mr. and Mrs. Davenport after this were in no way remarkable, except sadly remarkable that so great an actor should have been forced, in the greatest city of the Union, to play Hamlet to such poor houses and with such uncongenial surroundings.

On the evening of August 30, 1875, Mr. Davenport appeared as Hamlet in the Grand Opera-house, New York. On the same evening Barry Sullivan, under the management of Jarrett & Palmer, made his appearance at Booth's Theatre in the same part. The comparison invited by the presentation of these rival Hamlets was not favorable to the Irish tragedian. He was extensively advertised, and his reception by his own countrymen was affectionate and sincere. The Irish regiment, the famous Sixty-ninth, was present on the opening night, and the house was crowded with our Irish citizens. The performance was superior to the general run of Hamlets, but it was not superlative. Mr. Sullivan had had great experience on the British stage, and was skilled in his profession, but his Hamlet was melodramatic, harsh at times, occasionally overacted, and in all respects totally different from the quiet, tender Hamlet of Mr. Davenport. Much of his business was believed to be new, and some of his novelties were effective, if not altogether according to the text of the tragedy. It was a Hamlet that appealed to the taste of the audiences of the Bowery rather than to those of the west side of the town. It is only just to say that Hamlet was not Mr. Sullivan's strongest part in America. As Richard III., as Beverly, in *The Gamester*, and as Richelieu, he appeared to advantage, although his success in this country was not as great as his reputation at home would have warranted. This was his second appearance in America. His first was made at the Broadway Theatre, New York, and in the character of Hamlet, on the 22d of November, 1858.

The student of dramatic history in America must have been struck with the irregularity of the appearance of Hamlet upon our boards during the last hundred years. In Joseph Norton Ireland's *Records of the New York Stage*, published in 1866-67, and the best and most complete work of its kind in this country, and perhaps in any country, there are seasons and successions of seasons in which there is to be found no hint of its production; in other seasons some domestic or imported star was seen in the tragedy, for a night or two at most, on its meteoric flight from horizon to horizon, while, on the other hand, for months together *Hamlet* was of weekly if not of nightly occurrence at some of the theatres of the metropolis.

Probably at no period in the history of *Hamlet*, since the early days when Shakspere himself, according to tradition, played havoc with the Ghost, has any town witnessed such an epidemic of *Hamlet* as passed over the city of New York in the years

1857 and 1858. McKean Buchanan and Barry
Sullivan appeared as Hamlet at the Broadway,
James Stark and the elder Wallack at Wallack's,
Edward Eddy at the Bowery, and John Milton
Hengler, a rope-dancer, played Hamlet, "for one
night only," at Burton's, followed at that house by
Charles Carroll Hicks, James E. Murdoch, Edward
L. Davenport, and Edwin Booth.

The Hamlet of Edwin Booth, without doubt, is the
most familiar and the most popular in America to-
day. He has played the part in every important town
in the Union, many hundreds of nights in New York
alone, and to hundreds of thousands of persons, the
warmest of his admirers and most constant
attendants at his performances being men and
women who are emphatically non-theatre-goers,
and who never enter a play-house except to see Mr.
Booth, and Mr. Booth in a Shaksperian part. He has
done very much more than any other actor to
educate the popular taste to a proper understanding
of Hamlet, and to a proper appreciation of the
beauties of the tragedy. He is the ideal Hamlet of
half the people of the country who have any idea of
Hamlet whatever.

In many minds Booth *is* Hamlet, and Hamlet is
Booth; any conception of Hamlet that is not
Booth's, any picture of Hamlet which does not
resemble the familiar features of Booth, any
representation of Hamlet on the stage which is not
an imitation of Booth's Hamlet, is considered no
Hamlet at all. If the very Hamlet of tradition
himself--the Amleth of the old Danish legend from
which Shakspere drew, no doubt, the facts and

fancies of his play--were to return to earth and walk the boards of an American theatre, he would find no followers if he walked not, looked not, spoke not after the manner of Edwin Booth.

Mr. Booth's Hamlet is original in many respects; it is intellectual, intelligent, carefully studied, complete to the smallest details, and greatly to be admired. Nature has given him the melancholy, romantic face, the magnetic eye, the graceful person, the stately carriage, the poetic temperament, which are in so marked a degree characteristic of Hamlet, while his genius in many scenes of the tragedy carries him far above any of the Hamlets this country has seen in many generations of plays.

He first assumed the part in New York, and under Mr. Burton's management, at the Metropolitan Theatre, in the month of May, 1857. The engagement was short, and *Hamlet* was presented two or three times. Even then, however, it created no little excitement, and was considered a very remarkable and finished representation in a young man but twenty-four years of age. In Mr. Burton's company that season were Charles Fisher, Mark Smith, Thomas Placide, Sarah Stevens, Mrs. Hughes, and Mr. Burton himself, by whom the young tragedian was ably supported.

Mr. Booth next appeared in New York on the 26th of November, 1860, at the same theatre--then called the Winter Garden--under the management of William Stuart. He opened as Hamlet, and had the support of Miss Ada Clifton as Ophelia, of Mrs. Duffield as the Queen, and of Mr. Davidge and J. H.

Stoddart as the Grave-diggers. This was his first
genuine metropolitan success in the part, although it
was presented but five times during an engagement
of four weeks. A year or two later he played Hamlet
to the Ophelia of Mrs. Barrow; in 1863 he was
supported by Lawrence Barrett, Humphrey Bland,
"Dolly" Davenport, Vining Bowers, and Miss
Clifton; and still at the Winter Garden he appeared
as Hamlet from the 26th of November, 1864, until
the 24th of March, 1865, one hundred consecutive
nights! This was an event entirely unprecedented in
the history of *Hamlet* in any country, and probably
the longest run that any *tragedy* whatever had at
that time enjoyed. It was before the days of
Rosedale and *Led Astray*--before managers dared to
present a single play during an entire season, when
changes of bill were of weekly if not of nightly
occurrence, and when Mr. Booth himself, during an
engagement of fifteen or eighteen nights, had
played twelve or fifteen parts. "One hundred nights"
of any production is no novelty now, since *Adonis*
and *Erminie* have, with such little merit, drawn such
full houses for so many months; but that one man
should have played but this one part, and that too in
a drama so decidedly a one-man play that *Hamlet*
with Hamlet left out has become a proverb
wherever English is known, was a quarter of a
century ago certainly a magnificent achievement. It
moved Mr. Booth's many friends in New York to
present to him on the 22d of January, 1867, the
celebrated "Hamlet Medal," the most
complimentary and well-merited testimonial that
any young actor, no matter how brilliant his career,
has ever received from the American public in the
history of its stage. During this famous engagement

he was associated with Thomas Placide as Grave-
digger; with Charles Kemble Mason, an admirable
Ghost; with Charles Walcot, Jr., as Horatio; with
Owen Fawcett as Osric; with Mrs. James W.
Wallack, Jr., as the Queen; and with Mrs. Frank
Chanfrau as Ophelia--as strong a combination of
talent as the tragedy has often seen.

It is not possible to tell here the story of Mr. Booth's
many productions of *Hamlet* in New York, nor to
do more than barely enumerate the ladies and
gentlemen who have supported him. Among his
Ophelias, not mentioned above, have been Miss
Effie Germon (in 1866), Mme. Scheller, Miss
Blanche De Bar, Miss Bella Pateman, Miss
Jeffreys-Lewis, Miss Eleanor Carey, Mrs. Alexina
Fisher Baker, Miss Clara Jennings, Miss Minna
Gale, and Mme. Helena Modjeska. He has snubbed
and stabbed John Dyott, David C. Anderson,
Charles Fisher, and George Andrews, as Polonius.
His Grave-diggers have been Robert Pateman,
Charles Peters, and Owen Fawcett. Newton
Gothold, J. H. Taylor, David W. Waller, H. A.
Weaver, Charles Barron, Charles Kemble Mason,
and Lawrence Barrett have been his Ghosts, and
Mrs. Marie Wilkins, Miss Mary Wells, Mrs. Fanny
Morant, and Miss Ida Vernon, in their turn, have
been the mothers who his father had much
offended.

Lawrence Barrett, now so intimately associated
with Mr. Booth throughout the United States, has
played every male part in *Hamlet* with the exception
of Polonius and the First Grave-digger. His earliest
appearance in the tragedy was in Newcastle,

Pennsylvania, in 1855, when he represented the
leading character in a version of the play announced
on the bills as "The Grave Burst; or, The Ghost's
Piteous Tale of Horror, by W. Shakspere, Esqr."
The elaborate title was supposed to be more taking
with the theatre-going population of that particular
town than the simple name by which it is usually
known to Shaksperian students; but it is not
recorded that the representation was popular, or that
box receipts were in proportion to the outlay. Mr.
Barrett played Laertes to the Hamlet of Miss
Cushman, in Boston, some years later; he has been
the Ghost to the Hamlet of Edwin Booth and
Edward L. Davenport; and he has supported Barry
Sullivan, Mr. Murdoch, and other leading
tragedians at different seasons, taking the part of
Horatio to Mr. Murdoch's Hamlet, John
McCullough's Ghost, and Miss Clara Morris's
Queen, at the famous festival at Cincinnati a few
years ago. The fact that Mr. Barrett rarely plays
Hamlet in New York is much to be regretted. In
other cities, where he is better known in the part, he
is greatly liked, and next to his Cassius it is perhaps
the best thing he does. That it is a highly intellectual
performance goes without saying, but it has other
merits as well. It is vigorous, consistent, and
unfailingly tender.

Mr. Bandmann played Hamlet in German, and of
course with a German company, at the Stadt
Theatre in the Bowery, just at the close of the first
century of *Hamlet* in New York. He attracted a
great deal of attention among the German
population of the city, and was so successful in it
that it tempted him to study for the English-

speaking stage. He presented considerable business
that was new here, but well known in his fatherland, bringing his Ghost from beneath the stage,
introducing a manuscript copy of the speeches of
the actors in the play scene, and turning its leaves
back and forth in a restless way to hide the
nervousness of Hamlet. This was subsequently
noticed here in the performances of Mr. Fechter.
Mr. Bandmann also drew from his pouch tablets
upon which he set down the some dozen or sixteen
lines to be introduced by the First Actor in the
incident of the murder of Gonzago; and at the end
of the scene he fell back into the arms of Horatio in
a state of complete collapse. His acting throughout
was effective and powerful.

The Hamlet of Salvini is powerful but not effective.
It is not the Hamlet of tradition, nor does it overtop
the traditional Hamlet in novelty and originality. If
Salvini had played nothing but Hamlet here he
never could have sustained the magnificent
reputation he brought from foreign countries, and
which he more than fulfilled in other parts. The man
who excels as Ingomar, is superb as Samson,
supreme in Othello, and, in the entirely opposite
character of Sullivan (David Garrick), displays such
marked comedy powers, can hardly be expected to
shine as the melancholy Dane.

Rossi's Hamlet is effective if not powerful. In his
first interview with the Ghost he betrays no fear,
because he sees in it only the image of a lamented
and beloved father, while in the scene with the
Queen, when the Ghost appears, he crouches behind
his mother's chair in abject terror, because, as he

explains it, the phantom is then an embodiment of conscience, the Ghost of a father whose mandate he has disobeyed.

Unquestionably the imported Hamlet that has excited the greatest interest in New York in very many seasons is the Hamlet of Charles Fechter. The acting of no man, native or foreign, in the whole history of the American stage has been the subject of so much or of such varied criticism as his. There was no medium whatever concerning him in public opinion. Those who were his admirers were wildly enthusiastic in his praise; those who did not like him did not like him at all, and were unsparing in their condemnation and their ridicule; but no one was wholly indifferent to his acting. He came to this country endorsed by the strongest of letters from Charles Dickens, who was his friend, and weighted by the wholesale and impolitic puffery of his managers; the result was that, in the judgment of the majority of those who saw him, he did not and could not sustain the magnificent reputation claimed for him in his advance advertisements. On the other hand, while he was in a manner snubbed by New York, he was hailed in Boston as the Roscius of the nineteenth century. His Hamlet, although very uneven and unequal, was certainly a marvellous performance, and while by reason of date it does not come within the scope of the present chapter, it is too important in many ways to be omitted. It was thoroughly untraditional. He gave to the Prince of Denmark the fair Saxon face and the light flowing hair of the Danes of to-day; in his own portly form he made the too, too solid flesh of Hamlet a real rather than an ideal feature of

Hamlet's person: and much of his business, if not
original with him, was at least unfamiliar to
American play-goers. He was peculiarly "intense"
in everything he did, while in what are called the
intense scenes of the tragedy he was often more
subdued and natural even than Mr. Davenport, who
was remarkably free from emotional acting. His
"rest, perturbèd spirit," was excellent and effective
by reason of its very quietness, and during all of the
scene with the Ghost his acting was conspicuous by
the absence of the conventional quivering,
trembling, teeth-chattering agony which is so apt to
be the result of the coming of the apparition. In the
"rat-trap" and closet scenes, in which Mr. Booth is
so good, so very excellent good, Mr. Fechter lacked
dignity and repose; and in his advice to the players,
while his reading was less distinct and intelligent
than Mr. Booth's, his facial expression was
wonderful and beyond all praise. He was inferior to
Booth in the soliloquies, although charmingly
tender in his intercourse with Ophelia. With the
Queen in "the closet scene" he was almost brutal in
his conduct, seeming to forget entirely--what Mr.
Booth never overlooks--that Gertrude, although
sinning, is still a woman and his own mother. He
stabbed poor Polonius with a ferocity that destroyed
all sympathy for Hamlet. His reading, apart from
the accentuations and inflections which were
natural to him at all times, was peculiar; his
enunciation was frequently so rapid that it became
unintelligible; he hurried through some of the finest
passages at a gallop, and lost some of the finest
points; but his Hamlet as a whole was impressive
and magnetic, the oftener seen the better liked. Mr.
Fechter made his first appearance in America as

Ruy Blas at Niblo's Garden, New York, on the 10th
of January, 1870, under the management of Jarrett
& Palmer; and he played Hamlet for the first time
on the 15th of February the same year.

Among the purely exotic Hamlets of the New York
stage Salvini, Bandmann, Bogumil-Dawison, Rossi,
Barnay, and Hasse have been the most prominent.
But while the performance of each was excellent in
its own fashion, each labored under the great
disadvantage of playing a most familiar part (and in
a play decidedly an English classic) in a foreign
tongue.

It is not possible, of course, in the limits of a single
chapter to speak at any length of all the hundreds of
Hamlets who have appeared upon the New York
stage between the years 1761 and 1861, or to refer
to the scores of men who have played the part in
other cities. The following alphabetical list of those
who have been seen upon the metropolitan stage is
compiled from Mr. Ireland's *Records*, and from
many files of old play-bills in various collections,
and is felt to be fairly complete. It does not include
the tragedians whose performances have been
noticed elsewhere in the text of the present chapter,
or those who have played Hamlet in other cities of
the Union but not in New York; and the date
appended is that of the player's first recorded
appearance in the part here:

William Abbott, April 9, 1836; Augustus A.
Addams, November 13, 1835; J. R. Anderson,
September 3, 1844; George J. Arnold, 1854; Mr.
Barton, March 9, 1831; Mr. Bartow, May 26, 1815;

John Wilkes Booth, March, 1861; Frederick Brown, March 9, 1819; McKean Buchanan, June 10, 1850; Samuel Butler, November 4, 1841; John H. Clarke, November 8, 1822; Mr. Clason, November 10, 1824; G. F. Cooke (not the great George Frederick), October 4, 1839; Mr. Dunbar, December, 1813; Edward Eddy, August 27, 1852; Henry I. Finn, September 12, 1820; W. C. Forbes, May 29, 1833; Richard Graham, October 29, 1850; H. P. Grattan, May 11, 1843; James H. Hackett, October 21, 1840; Charles Carroll Hicks, December 13, 1858; Henry Erskine Johnstone, December, 1837; William Horace Keppell, November 17, 1831; H. Loraine, December 23, 1856; W. Marshall, February 3, 1848; J. A. J. Neafie, 1856; John R. Oxley, August 16, 1836; William Pelby, January 6, 1827; Charles Dibdin Pitt, November 8, 1847; J. B. Roberts, May 17, 1847; John R. Scott, March, 1836; James Stark, September, 1852; John Vandenhoff, October 2, 1837; Henry Wallack, September 4, 1824; James William Wallack, Jr., July, 1844; Wilmarth Waller, June 30, 1851.

As the limits of space here prevent more than the enumeration of the names of many men who were excellent Hamlets during the first century of its history in New York, so does the very nature of the article preclude any mention of the excellent Hamlets who have appeared in the part since the century closed in 1862, and who may be still alive. These no doubt will receive the attention of some later historian, who will do full justice to the Hamlets of the present and the future, from Henry Irving to N. S. Wood.

When George Henry Lewes, in "An Epistle to Anthony Trollope," made the bold assertion that "no actor has been known utterly to fail as Hamlet," he forgot four classes of actors whom perhaps he did not consider actors at all. These are, first, the infant prodigies; second, the ladies who attempt the part; third, the men who burlesque it; and fourth, the men who fail not only as Hamlet but as everything else. Of the first, something has already been said; of the second, something is yet to be said; of the third, William Mitchell, William E. Burton, and George L. Fox knew no such word as fail; and of the fourth, George the Count Johannes, in his later days, was a brilliant example. His occasional productions of *Hamlet* for his own benefit, a few years ago, were the source of much silly amusement and rude horse-play upon the part of audiences not wise enough to appreciate the mental condition of the unfortunate star, or their own want of taste in encouraging his buffoonery even by their ridicule. His support, composed entirely of amateurs, was without question the worst that any Hamlet has ever known in this country; but his own performance was neither good enough to be worthy of any notice whatever, nor bad enough to be funny.

The connection of George Jones with the American stage as a professional actor dates back to the early days of the Bowery Theatre. He made his American *début* there as the Prince of Wales in *Henry IV.*, on the 4th of March, 1831. He played Hamlet at the National Theatre in December, 1836, and he repeated the part (before he became too mad to portray even the mad prince) many times, not only in this country but in England. The last occasion

which merits even a passing word being at the
Academy of Music, New York, on the 30th of
April, 1864, when he was associated with Mrs.
Brougham (Robertson) as Ophelia, and Mrs.
Melinda Jones as the Queen.

The first record of any attempt to burlesque Hamlet
in New York is contained in the advertisements of
the Anthony (Worth) Street Theatre, June 13, 1821,
when Mr. Spiler was announced to play the Dane
and Mrs. Alsop Ophelia, "in the original travestie."
Mrs. Alsop's sudden death before the opening night
postponed the performance indefinitely, and it is not
known now when the travesty was produced, or if it
was produced at all that season. Mr. William
Mitchell presented Poole's absurd burlesque of the
tragedy at the Olympic Theatre on the 13th of
February, 1840, playing Hamlet himself. This, by
the graybeards who prate of the palmy days of the
drama--palmy meaning anything that is past--was
said to have been a finer performance than the
burlesque Hamlet of George L. Fox thirty years
later. At the New National Theatre--formerly the
Chatham--Mr. Frank Chanfrau played Hamlet after
the manner of Mr. Macready, October, 1848, in an
entertainment called *Mr. McGreedy*. But the
burlesque *Hamlet* which was most complete in all
its parts, unquestionably, was that produced at
Burton's Theatre in the season of 1857-58, when
John Brougham played Hamlet with a brogue;
Burton the Ghost; Dan Setchell Laertes; Lawrence
Barrett Horatio; and Mark Smith Ophelia.
Brougham had played the part previously at his own
Lyceum in 1851, and at the Bowery in 1856, but
never with such phenomenal support.

On the long file of the bills of *Hamlet* upon the New York stage the name of a lady is occasionally found in the titular part. The most daring and successful of these mongrel Hamlets was unquestionably Miss Charlotte Cushman--but even the genius of a Cushman was not great enough to crown the effort with success. In the early days of her career Miss Cushman had played the Queen in the tragedy to the Hamlet of James William Wallack the younger, at the National Theatre, New York, in April, 1837, and in the autumn of the same year to the Hamlet of Forrest at the Park. There is no record of her appearance as Ophelia. She played Hamlet for the first time in New York at Brougham's Lyceum, November 24, 1851, and she trod in the footsteps of Mrs. Bartley, who was seen as Hamlet at the Park, March 29, 1819; of Mrs. Barnes, who was seen in the same part on the same stage in June of the same year; of Mrs. Battersby, who played it May 22, 1822; and of Mrs. Shaw--whose Ghost was Mr. Hamblin--in April, 1839. Mrs. Brougham (Robertson) played Hamlet for her benefit in 1843, and so did Miss Fanny Wallack in 1849. This last lady frequently attempted the part, and at the Astor Place Opera-house, June 8, 1850, she had the support of Charles Kemble Mason as the Ghost and Miss Lizzie Weston as Ophelia. Other lady Hamlets have been Miss Marriott, Miss Clara Fisher, Mrs. Emma Waller, Miss Anna Dickinson, Mrs. Louise Pomeroy, Miss Rachel Denvil, Miss Susan Denin, Mrs. F. B. Conway, Miss Adele Belgarde, and finally Miss Julia Seaman, an English actress of fine figure, who played the Devil in the spectacle of *The White Fawn* at Niblo's Garden, and who succeeded in doing as much with Hamlet at Booth's Theatre in

1874.

The best actors in the world, either for tragedy, comedy, history, pastoral, pastoral-comical, historical-pastoral, scene individable, or poem unlimited, have been in Hamlet's train upon the New York stage since "first from England he was here arrived," so many years ago; but so much has been said of Hamlet that even the names of his most beautiful Ophelias, his honest Ghosts, his gentle Guildensterns, his aunt-mothers, his uncle-fathers, his wretched, rash, intruding Polonii, or the absolute knaves who have digged his Ophelia's grave--and lied in it--for a hundred years, cannot be enumerated here, except when they have played Hamlet himself, or have done as somebody else some wonderful things to Hamlet.

William Davidge related in his *Footlight Flashes* that during his strolling days in England, when companies were small, he had on the same evening done duty for Polonius, the Ghost, Osric, and the First Grave-digger; and Edwin Booth remembers Thomas Ward dying in sight of the audience as the Player King, and being dragged from the mimic stage by the heels to enter immediately at another wing as Polonius, with a cry of "Lights! lights! lights!" Hamlet, in a "one-night town," swearing that he loved Ophelia better than forty thousand brothers, has watched her through an open grave packing her trunk in the place beneath, while the Ghost, her husband, waited to strap it up! There are more things in Hamlet's existence--behind the scenes--than are dreamed of in the philosophy of all his commentators and all his critics.

One of the most notable instances of a great actor
assuming a small part was on the occasion of
Charles Kean's first appearance as Hamlet in
Baltimore, when at the Holiday Street Theatre, in
1831, the elder Booth, at that time at the very height
of his fame and prosperity, for some reason now
unknown, volunteered to play the Second Actor, the
most insignificant character in the tragedy. John
Duff was the Ghost; Mrs. Duff Queen Gertrude;
John Sefton Osric; Thomas Flynn First Grave-
digger; and William Warren, father of the William
Warren for whom Boston mourns to-day, was
Polonius. This was an exceedingly strong cast of the
tragedy, and the Second Actor most certainly was
never in better hands on any stage.

The strongest cast of *Hamlet*, in all its parts, ever
presented in America, was that at the famous
Wallack Testimonial in New York, on the 21st of
May, 1888, when Lawrence Barrett played the
Ghost; Frank Mayo the King; John Gilbert
Polonius; Eben Plympton Laertes; John A. Lane
Horatio; Joseph Wheelock the First Actor; Milnes
Levick the Second Actor; Henry Edwards the
Priest; Joseph Jefferson and William J. Florence the
Grave-diggers; Miss Kellogg Gertrude; Miss
Coghlan the Player Queen; and Madame Modjeska
Ophelia to the Hamlet of Edwin Booth.

The first record of any performance of *Hamlet* in
New York, as has been shown, was at the theatre in
Chappel Street, November 26, 1761. On the 26th of
November, 1861, Mr. Booth played the same part at
the Winter Garden, on Broadway. The coincidence
was not noticed at the time, and no doubt was

purely accidental. It was a very pleasant coincidence, nevertheless, and it is certainly a happy fact that Edwin Booth should have been selected by chance to celebrate upon the New York stage the centenary of *Hamlet* in New York.

CURTAIN.

Printed in Great Britain
by Amazon

38125313R20095